THRIVING HACKS
Simple Hacks For a Richer, Healthier and Fulfilling Life

RAVIKUMMAR M

STARDOM BOOKS

STARDOM BOOKS

WORLDWIDE

www.StardomBooks.com

STARDOM BOOKS

A Division of Stardom Publishing

and infoYOGIS Technologies.

105-501 Silverside Road

Wilmington, DE 19809

Copyright © 2021 by Ravikummar M

All rights reserved, including right to reproduce
this book or portions thereof in any form whatsoever.

FIRST EDITION SEPTEMBER 2021

Stardom Books

Thriving Hacks/
Simple Hacks For a Richer, Healthier
and Fulfilling Life

Ravikummar M

p. 268
cm. 15.24 X 22.86

Category: Self-Help/Personal
Growth/Success (SEL027000)

ISBN: 978-1-7369486-4-4

DEDICATION

To my mother Anasuyamma, who is my first teacher and who cares more about her children than herself. To my father Late Somashekharappa, who taught me the power of discipline and focus.

To my wife Malini, who taught me patience and perseverance.
To my daughter Neetu, my youngest and brightest teacher.

To my sisters Asha and Sujatha, who always stood by me as my strength.

To all my teachers who taught me lessons throughout my life; specifically Late Jim Rohn, Jack Canfield, Bob Proctor and Mani Subramanian who reshaped my life and my outlook towards life.

And, finally, my dear readers.
I sincerely hope you'll understand the idea behind this book — I would be the happiest if even a handful of you embrace the teachings mentioned in this book.

CONTENTS

	Acknowledgments	i
	Foreword	iii
	WHY I WROTE THIS BOOK?	1
	INTRODUCTION – HOW TO USE THIS BOOK?	3
	LIVING WITH INTENT	
1	FINDING YOUR LIFE PURPOSE	9
2	SETTING A GRAND VISION FOR YOUR LIFE	13
3	SETTING AND ACHIEVING GOALS	17
	LIVING IN ALIGNMENT	
4	WHEN GOALS ARE NOT ENOUGH	23
5	GETTING IN THE FLOW	25
6	USING THE LAW OF ATTRACTION	29
7	CULTIVATING THE ABUNDANCE MINDSET	33
	BEING YOUR BEST SELF	
8	BEING AN IDEA MACHINE	41
9	BEING PRODUCTIVE	45
10	INTEGRITY IS THE WAY OF LIFE	51

11	MASTERING YOUR HABITS	55
12	MINDING YOUR WORDS	61
13	BEING ATTRACTIVE	65

TAKING CHARGE OF YOUR FINANCES

14	MONEY FUNDAMENTALS	71
15	SPEND VS. SAVE VS. INVEST	75
16	BEING ASSET-LIGHT	79
17	INCREASING YOUR EARNING POTENTIAL	83

TAKING CHARGE OF YOUR CAREER

18	THE CAREER CONUNDRUM	91
19	BEING VALUABLE	97
20	BEING SERVICE-MINDED	103
21	BEING A PROLIFIC PROFESSIONAL	109
22	BEING VISIBLE	113
23	DEVELOPING AN ENTREPRENEURIAL MINDSET	119
24	FUTURE-PROOFING YOURSELF	123

TAKING CHARGE OF YOUR HEALTH AND WELL-BEING

25	ENVIRONMENTAL POLLUTION AND TOXICITY	129
26	HOLISTIC HEALTH	133
27	DIET	137
28	GUT HEALTH	143

29	METABOLISM	147
30	FASTING AND AUTOPHAGY	151
31	HYDRATION	155
32	ACTIVE LIFESTYLE	159
33	SLEEP	163
34	MEDITATION	167
35	BREATHWORK	171
36	LONGEVITY AND ANTI-AGING	175

LIVING YOUR HIGHEST JOY

37	HAPPINESS AND FULFILLMENT	181
38	PRACTICING BENEFICIAL WORRYING	187
39	BEING SPONTANEOUS	191
40	BEING STILL	195
41	MAKING A DIFFERENCE	199
	Hacks ready-reckoner	203
	References	243
	Afterword	251
	About the author	253

ACKNOWLEDGMENTS

I'd like to take this opportunity to thank my friends and colleagues for teaching me the crucial life lessons all these years.
This book is the result of all those learnings.

Many thanks to Raam Anand and his team at Stardom Books for all their efforts in polishing the book, innumerable edits and thoughtful interventions in making this book a reality.

Lastly, I value and respect each and every one who has been a part of this book. If I have unknowingly missed out on acknowledging anyone's contributions, please know that your contribution is highly valued.

FOREWORD

I'm an avid reader of personal development. It helps me expand my personal growth so that I can reach my highest potential and help others do the same. After reading over a thousand books and attending many personal growth and business training sessions, there's one thing I appreciate the most in the entire learning process: The way the authors and trainers break down complex concepts into their simplest form and make them easily applicable and life-changing at the same time. Ravi does just that in this book.

In 2010, Ravi and I first met in Scottsdale, Arizona, at *Breakthrough to Success*, a transformative event led by Jack Canfield, co-creator of the billion-dollar brand "Chicken Soup for the Soul" and best-selling author of "The Success Principles." We then became graduates of Jack Canfield's *Train the Trainer* program the following year and have connected many times since then.

Whether it be Silicon Valley, Las Vegas, or Bengaluru, India, meeting Ravi has always been a profound and breakthrough experience for me. His encouraging words, kind spirit, and tips for success always elevate my thinking, which ultimately helps me break into new levels of my life. What I appreciate most about Ravi is that he genuinely cares about your success. He truly wants to see you succeed in all areas of your life.

Fortunately, through his many accomplishments and years of being a leader, Ravi has laid out many practical, bite-size hacks that can serve as a roadmap to help you reach your full potential while living a life you love. In this book, he shares concepts, exercises, and suggestions on finding your life purpose, setting a grand vision for your life, cultivating an abundance mindset, finding your flow, taking charge of your career, and much more.

Thriving Hacks **reminds me of three important messages:**

- You are meant not just to survive but to thrive.
- You are meant not just to reach your goals but to reach your full potential.
- You are meant not to wander wondering what the meaning of life is but to live a life with meaning and wonder.

I'm excited about what these hacks will bring you. Whether it's all 136 of them or just one, I know they will make a positive impact in your life so that you could live a life with purpose and passion.

It's time to hack away!

Believing in Your Greatness,
Romeo Marquez Jr.
International Speaker | Success Coach | Best-Selling Author
www.RomeoMarquezJr.com

WHY I WROTE THIS BOOK

Born to a middle-class family in southern India, I was raised by loving yet strict parents. Their approach to life was getting good grades, getting a job, and starting a family – very normal expectations.

I got my master's in manufacturing engineering with a specialization in Robotics. At the time, India was emerging as a destination for software engineering, and I found my way into this lucrative field. Like many budding Indian professionals, my dream was to get to the land of opportunity, America! I was fortunate to join a start-up in the US run by an ambitious founder, who groomed me to become a leader.

After ten years, my CEO asked if I was ready to return to India to do bigger and better things. Since then, I've had the responsibility and privilege of managing and interacting with tens of thousands of talented individuals. I became passionate about the "excellence in execution" concept. Although our teams succeeded at seemingly impossible tasks most of the time, there were instances when they failed to deliver on simple assignments!

As a manager and leader, I kept asking myself, "How do we get the best out of people consistently?" and "Why do people excel on some occasions and fail in others?" Looking for answers, I studied others and myself and concluded that the main reasons for failure were lack of clear thinking and the lack of 'burning' desire.

Eventually, I expanded my inquiry beyond the work arena to understand why very few people thrive in life while the majority meander. After a great deal of observation and contemplation, I feel that there are two reasons: First, they do not ask the crucial question, "What do I really want?" Second, even when they do, they are too busy earning a living to pursue their life's purpose. It may be glaringly obvious, but to reach our highest potential, we must be financially independent. To prosper, we must become valuable to the marketplace, and that starts with self-improvement.

The Quote That Changed My Life:

Several years ago, while preparing a presentation to a large group of new graduates on how to succeed in their careers, especially at our company, I stumbled on a powerful quote: **"We must all suffer from one of two pains: the pain of discipline or the pain of regret. The difference is discipline weighs ounces while regret weighs tons."**

Mesmerized by its profundity, my first thought was, "I wish I had this understanding ten years ago!" That was the first time I heard of Jim Rohn, and I have been his ardent student since. I have also studied and practiced principles taught by personal development legends like Bob Proctor, Brian Tracy, Zig Ziglar, Tony Robbins, and many others.

I have invested countless hours in the pursuit of becoming the best version of myself for the greater good, being aware that this never-ending undertaking is what makes life worth living.

I have shared my knowledge, hoping to improve the lives of those around me. With this book, I take the next step. Sure, there are countless personal development books, but I saw a need for practical, bite-size actions, "hacks," that everyone can take to improve their lives. Happy reading.

INTRODUCTION: HOW TO USE THIS BOOK

Having spent a considerable amount of time pondering what it takes to thrive in life, I admit that the requirements appear overwhelming. Unsurprisingly, many people do not have the time or energy to "figure it out." However, I am not deterred easily. Having led many teams to their professional best and worked hard on improving myself, I feel I am in a unique position to help. Simplifying, clarifying, and encapsulating the pursuit is my contribution with this book.

So, What Are *Thriving Hacks?*

It is a compendium of ideas, knowledge, and suggestions that you can stuff into your 'travel bag' as you begin your journey. Think of it as your roadmap to a more fulfilling life.

What is the Roadmap Comprised of?

The book takes you from life's biggest questions to practical aspects of everyday life and back to approaches that can make your health, heart, and mind soar. It begins by examining what it means and what it takes to live with intent. Questions, exercises, and suggestions help you seek your life purpose, envision the grandest vision for your life, and achieve your goals. The next section sheds light on the stumbling blocks to thrive and how to overcome them.

Why do we fail to achieve goals despite our hard work? How do we get in the flow? How to use the Law of Attraction and cultivate a mindset of abundance? Without integrating these knowledge and mindset shifts, the chances of living a fulfilling life are diminished.

The third section deals with how you present yourself to the world – how much your values, traits, habits, communication style, and productivity levels hinder or help you. The fourth section, packed with information and suggestions, helps you take charge of your finances. It teaches you money fundamentals, helps you increase your earning potential, minimize liabilities, and makes the most of your current resources.

Once you've learned the basics of money, the focus turns to your career. This section shows you how to increase your marketplace 'value' by being service-minded, developing an entrepreneurial approach, boosting your visibility and professionalism, and future-proofing yourself. The next section centers on physical, mental, and emotional health. It starts with basics like diet, gut health, metabolism, hydration, sleep, and moves on to powerful modalities like meditation and breathwork, and ends with longevity and youth.

The last section delves into happiness, fulfillment, spontaneity, stillness, and even beneficial worrying. The book closes as it begins—A big picture urging you to consider how you fit into the collective while making a difference in the world.

Don't exist.
Live.
Get out, explore.
Thrive.
Challenge authority. Challenge yourself.
Evolve.
Change forever.
– Brian Krans

How Should I Use *Thriving Hacks?*

First, read the book from beginning to end. Do your best not to skip chapters, even if you feel you have those areas "under control." The chapters are succinct, and you can always pick up something useful. Second, use the book as a 'how-to' guide. Start again at the beginning, creating a "thriving journal" where you record your answers, ideas, thoughts, and insights as you work through the questions and exercises. I urge you to research anything that pops out at you since that is the voice of your intuition prompting you to action.

Third, implement, implement, and implement. Shall I say that again? Implement! You can lead a horse to water, but if the horse does not drink and dies of thirst, who's to blame? Applying these principles to your life takes effort and discipline. As you use the suggestions in your everyday life, journal the process and progress – this will help you stay motivated.

Repeat exercises as needed, and revisit those you postponed. After some time, you may discover new insights and ways to apply these principles when you review your notes.

What Is the Takeaway?

I can't emphasize enough the fact that the entire book is a thriving hack. Yes, the roadmap appears long, winding, and multifaceted but are you not worth the effort? Do not treat this as a race; it takes time to integrate shifts in mindset, personality and lifestyle.

Make the changes slowly, bit-by-bit. Without a doubt, you will make gains every step of the way. If you have a burning desire to live with intent, in alignment with your life purpose, and experience your highest joy and potential, I am honored and humbled to contribute to your journey to thriving!

"Live less out of habit and more out of intent."

LIVE WITH INTENT

Harnessing the power of your mind for a more vivid life experience

"If you have a strong purpose in life, you don't have to be pushed. Your passion will drive you there."
– Roy T. Bennett

1

FINDING YOUR LIFE PURPOSE

"The soul which has no fixed purpose in life is lost; to be everywhere is to be nowhere."
– Michel de Montaigne

"Why do I exist?", "What is my life's purpose?"... are questions as old as humanity. They are the crux of all philosophical-spiritual exploration and are intrinsically tied to our awareness of our mortality. We go through life knowing we have an 'expiration date.' We tend to savor every moment and leave our mark on the world. In Maslow's hierarchy of needs, the highest level of psychological development is self-actualization. In this state, one achieves their potentialities (e.g., skills, talents), typically after having their basic needs met.

In other words, they fulfill their life purpose and thrive! Unfortunately, most of us live on 'autopilot' mode for various reasons. If we are in survival mode, then it becomes difficult to pursue our dreams – provided we even know what would bring us true joy. Also, fear gets in the way of our soul-searching. What if the answer to the question "Is my life meaningful and fulfilling?" is a resounding "no"? Yet, the Socratic wisdom, "The unexamined life is not worth living," is evergreen not only in every age but also at any age.

> *A 63-year-old woman named Laura Shultz managed to lift the backend of a Buick all by herself off the arm of her little grandson. This led to her meeting Dr. Charles Garfield, author of Peak Performers, who wanted to interview her about this amazing feat. Laura shared that since the incident, she had been asking herself, "If I was able to do this when I didn't think I could, what does that say about the rest of my life? Have I wasted it?" With Dr. Garfield's help, she discovered that it is never too late to make a change. Laura went to college, studied geology, and spent her golden years teaching at a community college.*

This story illustrates two things:

- First, we have almost unlimited untapped potential, like this Supergirl-strength in a 63-year-old lady, and second, it's never too late to ask, "Is this is how I want to spend my life?". It also shows that the energy of purpose makes all the difference.

Another reason we go through life on autopilot: When we ask, "What is my life purpose?" – we come up empty. Without direction, we get stuck on a hamster wheel of frustration, trial, and error, often propelled by other people's expectations and ideas, parents, peers, media, and so on. Driven by external needs, both real (making a living and raising a family) and false (keeping up with the latest trends or the Joneses), we lose our inner compass. Only by finding our 'true north' can we bring focus to our lives. Happiness, growth, and success will follow.

The fact that you have picked up this book proves you want to live with intent. You are ready to shake off the autopilot haze and shine your light onto the world. *"We are all meant to shine, / As children do. / We were born to make manifest / The glory of God that is within us. / It's not just in some of us; / It's in everyone,"* as the verses by Marianne Williamson so beautifully express.

Since the journey to thriving is guided by one's life purpose, the following exercise will help you bring **yourself** into focus. Who are you? What makes you happy? *"A musician must make music; an artist must paint; a poet must write, if he is to be ultimately happy,"* as Maslow describes self-actualization.

Hack 1: Exercise to Discover Your Life Purpose:

Get a pen and a piece of paper, and then set aside some alone time. Start by getting into a relaxed state, like going for a walk or meditating. The goal is to reduce the mind chatter and open up to deeper insights. When you feel centered, write each question at the top of the page, then jot down any answer that comes to mind. Don't worry if you can't answer fully or if the answer doesn't immediately make sense – this is not a race but a process. It may take several sessions before the picture starts to become clear.

a) **Which five adjectives would you use to define success?**
Complete the sentence in this way, "I am successful if I am/feel…" (e.g., peaceful, rich, attractive, respected, loved). Try not to rationalize or respond based on expectations, either yours or other people's—answer from your gut, feelings, and desires. By exploring your definition of success, you are essentially discovering your version of happiness, which is tied to your life purpose.

b) **Why are these five conditions important to you?**

Once you have defined what success means to you, the next step is to analyze why you feel this way. If one answer was "I am successful if I am rich," delve into how that idea was created. Did you grow up poor? Don't you have enough disposable income for luxuries? Do you want to be free of the 9-5 grind to travel? If you answer honestly, you will begin to see what you truly value. Only by acknowledging your innermost needs and desires can you discover your purpose.

c) **If you could live your life as another person, who would it be and why?**
A more indirect approach to the above questions makes it easier to bypass subconscious conditioning. Since this is an imaginary scenario, you are more likely to allow your true desires to surface. If you said, "I would like to be Beyoncé," delve into 'why.' It truly does not matter what Beyoncé's life is actually like. The only thing that matters is how you imagine it and why. Do you have an unfulfilled dream to sing? Do you want to be in the spotlight?

d) **At the end of your life, what things would you wish you had accomplished?**
Start by writing down your list of desired accomplishments, then switch perspective and ask, "Which three will still be meaningful to me at the end of my life?"
For example, instead of wealth, you are more likely to realize that spending time with loved ones was more fulfilling. Delve deeper by shifting perspective again, "If I continue living my life this way, what three things am I likely to regret on my death bed?"

e) **If someone were to write a book about you, what would you want your story to be?**
Dream big! Make it as grand as possible, "a pioneer explorer; discovered the cure for cancer; among the most gifted filmmakers of all time." The exercise will help you identify the things you wish to be remembered for, your legacy. However, your contribution to the world can be as simple and profound as, "A person who showed love, kindness, and generosity to everyone who crossed their path."

"You don't need to live by someone else's standards. Live your vision and demand your own success."

2

SETTING A GRAND VISION FOR YOUR LIFE

"...If you work hard enough and assert yourself, and use your mind and imagination, you can shape the world to your desires."
- Malcolm Gladwell in Outliers

World-renowned speaker, motivational coach, and my mentor Bob Proctor said this at one of the workshops I attended: "If you can tell me what you want, I will show you how to get it." His words had a profound impression on me – that was the day I realized that most people's lives are defined by circumstances, environment, and default choices. They drift to places they never intended to go in the ocean of life because they had not set a destination, vision, or purpose. They do not use their rudder!

Let's be 100% clear: The universe does not have a predefined plan for your life. It will bring all kinds of situations your way, but you have the free will and ability to reset your course.

Once you focus on your destination, the universal wheels go into motion to attract you towards it. Coincidence will help steer you in the desired direction, but action is required from you. Always! If you can choose any destination, why not do something magnificent? Why not create a worthwhile life? The larger-than-life people who have blessed this earth with their presence had a clear vision of what they wanted to achieve. By announcing it publicly, they made themselves accountable and gave others the chance to support them on their journey.

Let's Consider the Following Examples:

- Mahatma Gandhi – To create a non-violent society where there is a balance between individual freedom and social responsibility.
- John F. Kennedy – To put a man on the moon by the end of the decade.
- Elon Musk – To accelerate the world's transition to sustainable energy.
- Kiran Bedi – To reform India's criminal justice system.
- Greta Thunberg – To get governments to take climate change seriously and start acting on it.
- Malala Yusafzai – To give every girl the right to education.

How to Define the Vision for Your Life?

Even if you are unclear about your life purpose, you must set a vision for your life. It's imperative because – without a destination – you will waste time and energy drifting. What kind of life would you like to create for yourself? Make it as grand and majestic as you dare, knowing that it is not set in stone; you can always tweak it along the way.

The key to setting that vision is acting on your passion, values, and aptitudes. If you feel strongly about education, how could you make the most difference to your students? If you are passionate about sustainable agriculture, how could you contribute to that area? If you are an engineer, how could your work serve the people and the planet?

Most people scoff at the thought of setting a grand vision because they think it's too theoretical, just motivational mumbo-jumbo, and not practical. However, as we have seen, setting a destination is the only truly practical approach to life because it's the only way to get where you want to go.

If we dig deeper into people's resistance to dream big, we find a lack of self-confidence, feelings of helplessness, and the fear of failure. This is nothing about 'self-sabotage.' It is much easier to be average, blend in, and do what is expected of us.

Living big means going against the grain. We are paralyzed into non-action, cheating ourselves out of the best that life has to offer. Worse still, the path of least resistance is extremely unfulfilling; it is highly unlikely that we will live our purpose by following the herd.

Not everyone wants to change the world, and that's okay! Your vision can be as big or as small as you wish it to be. The important thing is that it is meaningful to you and inspires you to live your purpose while making a difference in the world.

I want to emphasize here that the vision you set for yourself today is not set in stone. You can adjust or change it as your thinking evolves and you develop more clarity – that's growth. The key is to begin now, with whatever you know at this moment. Here are some guidelines to help define your life vision:

Hack 2: Choose a Life-Spanning Goal:

Remember, this vision is aspirational. Ideally, it should give you a purpose for your whole life, perhaps even inspire others beyond your lifetime.

Hack 3: Choose Something Scary and Exciting:

If it's not daunting, you're thinking too small. If it's not exciting, you won't be able to keep working towards this goal for decades.

Hack 4: Choose Something That Fills You with Energy and Personal Power:

It should get you out of bed every morning. If it doesn't fill you with enthusiasm, then go back to the drawing board. Your vision should invigorate you enough to overcome obstacles and challenges because there will be plenty. You will need to get up, dust yourself off, and carry on.

Hack 5: Choose a Role Model:

You don't need to reinvent the wheel. There are many studies that have outlined what makes some people extraordinarily successful. Malcolm Gladwell's book *Outliers: The Story of Success* offers an excellent compilation. The following exercise will help you choose your role model:

- Make a list of three people you admire.
- List three aspects of each person that makes you admire them.
- Rank these nine aspects in the order of importance (for you).
- Pick the three that you feel are most important to you.

- Use these three qualities/aspects in one positive sentence to define your initial desire.
- Re-write this goal statement in your own words. Keep repeating and tweaking it until it feels aligned.
- Once you feel good about it, try it out with family and friends. When we say things aloud, they often feel quite different. Tweak and test until you settle on your goal.
- Give yourself permission to change it if you find that it's not right for you at some point.

Hack 6: Gain Clarity on Why You Want Something:

Find solitude and think, really think, especially before bed. Your subconscious will bring you insights during dreamtime.

The goal of this exercise is to come up with five reasons why you want that life vision. Write it over and over again. Make it yours.

Here is an example:

I want to be a musician because...

- I have loved singing ever since I can remember.
- I want to create music that mesmerizes the audience.
- I can reach millions of people with my message.
- Music is my way of conveying happiness, sadness, and true feelings to the world.
- Music is the highest form of creative expression for me, and I want to master it.
- Music is pure and speaks directly to the heart.

3

SETTING AND ACHIEVING GOALS

"Whenever you want to achieve something, keep your eyes open, concentrate and make sure you know exactly what it is you want. No one can hit their target with their eyes closed." – Paulo Coelho

Henry Ford once said, *"Thinking is the hardest part"* – this may be one reason why 95% of the world's population drifts through life. Knowing the desired destination is not enough; getting there requires action based on analysis and planning.

People do not strategize and wait for their proverbial "ship to come in." Needless to say, this typically results in failure, which leads to feelings of defeat, which prevents them from pursuing their dreams, which leads to more defeat, and so on. Breaking the cycle requires a realistic and actionable plan simply by setting goals.

Why do Goals fail?

Let's make two things perfectly clear: First, successful people are not necessarily smarter than the rest; second, setting goals does not guarantee success. Let's examine the reasons:

- **Postponement:** Begin working towards your objective right away, even if you are starting small. For example, if you can't afford to go to medical school, enroll in complementary healthcare courses. This may open a new path for you.
- **Goals based on circumstance:** As illustrated in the above example, goals based on circumstance are worthwhile as long as they move you closer to your destination.

However, feeling discouraged because you did not get into the university your family has always attended is a recipe for failure. Always forge your own path based on something that you desire wholeheartedly.

- **Goals based on impulse:** Most new year's resolutions fail because they are made with no plan. Unless you are ready to commit, you will likely fail, reinforcing the failure-defeat cycle and demoralizing you further.
- **No cohesive plan:** The action you take needs to follow a roadmap of realistic and attainable steps.

How To Create A Roadmap?

Like bricks in a building, any overall plan is composed of smaller goals. Here, we offer some advice on how to project-manage your life:

- **Information and inspiration:** Research how people who have achieved similar goals did it, drawing both information and inspiration. But, remember that everyone's journey is unique.
- **Have a solid foundation:** Everyone builds one brick at a time, starting from the bottom. You always need a solid foundation. For example, if you want to own a hotel, you need hotel management training or hire a professional for that position.
- **Analyze the steps:** Reverse-engineer your end goal and break it down into smaller objectives in terms of their sequence. Identify potential roadblocks, and think about how to overcome them. Here are some helpful questions to ask: Where am I today? Where do I want to end up? What steps do I need to take to get there? What help do I need?

- **Be flexible:** Situations are fluid. Some redirection may be required. Be flexible and open to new approaches. If you encounter an obstacle, it may have a silver lining that reveals a better path.
- **Listen to your gut instinct.** Working toward a goal is a focused process, as well as an opportunity for self-discovery. Don't be rigid in your thinking or overly rational; allow your intuition to offer insights and inspiration. Emotional intelligence accounts for 80-90% of success, so make the most of it.

Hence, have a roadmap with a clear destination comprised of smaller objectives. The following suggestions will help you set and achieve your goals:

Hack 7: Set SMART Goals:

In *Attitude Is Everything: If You Want to Succeed Above and Beyond*, Paul J. Meyer describes a system for setting goals he calls 'SMART,' the acronym for Specific, Measurable, Achievable, Relevant, Time-bound. Let's get a better understanding.

- **Specific:** Your goal should be clear and specific; otherwise, you won't be able to focus your efforts. When drafting your goal, answer the following questions: What do I want to accomplish? Who is involved? Which resources are required? What are the limits?
- **Measurable:** Assessing your progress helps you meet deadlines and stay motivated. If your goal is measurable, you should be able to answer such questions: How much? How many? How will I know when it is accomplished?
- **Achievable:** To determine whether a goal is attainable, answer the following questions: How can I accomplish this goal? How realistic is it considering the various constraints?
- **Relevant:** This step ensures that the goal aligns with your roadmap and grand vision for your life. If it is, you should be able to answer 'yes' to such questions: Does it seem worthwhile? Is this the right time? Does this complement my other efforts/needs? Am I the right person to reach this goal? Is it applicable in the current socio-economic environment?
- **Time-bound:** Every goal needs a target date to prevent postponement and delays. You should be able to answer these questions: When is the earliest I can achieve this? What can I do to move forward today? What can I do six weeks from now? What can I do six months from now?

Hack 8: Objectives and Key Results (OKR):

This framework helps organizations define objectives and track results. The concept was created by Andy Grove, popularized by John Doerr, and used in Google, LinkedIn, Twitter, Dropbox, Spotify, Airbnb, and Uber. It is based on finding measurable and verifiable markers for lofty goals and can be applied to one's personal life.

Set the objective (what you want to accomplish) and the key results (how you will achieve it). For example, John Doerr wanted to spend more quality time with his family. He broke down his objective into two KRs:

- One, the whole family would have dinner together twenty nights a month. Two, the family would have no access to the internet during such gatherings.

Hack 9: Have an Accountability Partner:

Find someone you respect who is equally goal-oriented – a mentor, life coach, or friend. Discuss your progress regularly – talking about your goals makes your KRs more tangible and keeps you motivated.

LIVE IN ALIGNMENT
Harnessing the power of your mind for a more organized life experience

"If you align expectations with reality, you will never be disappointed."
- Terrel Owens

4

WHEN GOALS ARE NOT ENOUGH

The mind has a powerful way of attracting things that are in harmony with it, good and bad." – Idowu Koyenikan

The journey to thriving begins by focusing our vision, passion, and efforts in a clear direction- by living with an intent. As crucial as that is, it's only step one; step two is living in alignment. Many people do not reach their goals despite working diligently towards them. While it's easy to brush off failure when it's a spur-of-the-moment New Year's resolution, it can be soul-crushing when you do your best to no avail. Let's explore this unpleasant scenario to see what lies at the root of the problem.

When Nothing Works Out:

"When defeat comes, accept it as a signal that your plans are not sound, rebuild those plans, and set sail once more toward your coveted goal," said Napoleon Hill. In many cases, failure points simply to the need for a new strategy. However, the hidden message may also be that we are not in alignment in the following ways:

- **Life Purpose, Highest Good:**

Failing despite extensive efforts may indicate that we are not working towards our life purpose. Yes, free will enables us to make misaligned choices and mistakes. However, the Law of Cause and Effect is unwavering – every action produces a result, good or bad. For example, setting a professional goal that does not serve our highest personal growth is like eating junk and ending up with lifestyle diseases.

Sometimes, we think we know what we are meant to do in life – influenced by social conditioning – but that's not our path. Even if we achieve our goals, we may end up feeling empty. Remember the exercise of imagining what would be important to you on your deathbed?

- **Negative Thought Patterns:**

In addition to being out of alignment with our life purpose, some mental processes, usually subconscious, thwart success. Are you sabotaging yourself with your thoughts, feelings, and beliefs? This is where the Law of Attraction and the Law of Abundance come into play. You may be doing all the right things, but if your default mindset is focused on lack and negativity, the path will likely be fraught with frustration and failure because you create your reality with your thoughts.

When Things Fall into Place:

Life seems to work out for a few lucky people miraculously. They appear to stumble on opportunities and trip over success. The first question is, why? The second question is, how to be like them? The answer may be simple but not necessarily easy to apply to one's life since it requires internal shifts.

Without knowing it, as it's typically second nature to them, the so-called "lucky ones" use the universal laws to their benefit. As a result, they swim downstream and get carried to their desired destination by the river's flow. They are living in alignment with their purpose. In my view, the inner work is more important than the outer work, meaning, setting goals is often not enough. Nevertheless, in mapping the road to thriving in this book, I began with things that most people readily understand – purpose, intent, goals, and action – because they are tangible. Moreover, they are fundamental. In the following chapters, we will explore how to live in alignment.

5

GETTING IN THE FLOW

"There is an ecstasy that marks the summit of life, and beyond which life cannot rise. And such is the paradox of living, this ecstasy comes when one is most alive, and it comes as a complete forgetfulness that one is alive." – Jack London

Is there any doubt that some people are born for certain vocations? Child prodigies, science geniuses, and brilliant artists are so much in harmony with their life purpose and gifts that they make demanding tasks seem effortless – that's because they are "in the zone."

The phrase originated from NBA coach Phil Jackson, who worked with players like Michael Jordan and Kobe Bryant, but the concept was nothing new; it's as old as humanity.

Running guru Jim Fixx spoke of "the runner's high"– elation, coupled with diminished anxiety and pain, produced by a release of endorphins when the body is pushed to its limits. Psychiatrist Abraham Maslow described the "peak experience," a performance at the best level of a person's physical and/or cognitive abilities. All these expressions and terms point to the "flow state of mind," which was studied by positive psychologists Mihaly Csikszentmihalyi and Jeanne Nakamura.

Nothing could be further from the truth than assuming that this is the privilege of great talent. We all experience this feeling many times in our lives – when we play like children, when we are in love, and when we are doing something we love. However, some factors set such leaders apart.

The first difference is they experience the flow more often, simply because they are doing what they were born to do. The second difference is that they know how to produce it on demand. It's not enough to be in the zone at random moments in highly competitive or demanding fields. A pro athlete must bring their "A-game" to the arena practically every time.

Even if you never compete in the Olympics, you need to learn how to reach peak performance at will to thrive in life. Lasting success is a product of repeated peak performances.

Understanding the Flow and Its Benefits:

Positive psychology describes the flow as the mental state in which a person is fully immersed in energized focus, involvement, and enjoyment of activity – composing music, writing, etc. The mad scientist's caricature, who is so preoccupied with his research that he forgets to sleep or groom himself, is an exaggerated but truthful illustration.

The flow can be likened to a deep meditative state or heightened euphoric daze, where the person is fully active and present. Time, hunger, thirst, fatigue, and even pain can fade away, replaced by deep focus, dedication, and fulfillment. According to Csikszentmihalyi, "The best moments in our lives usually occur if a person's body or mind is stretched to its limits in a voluntary effort to accomplish something difficult and worthwhile."

What are the benefits of this state, and why should you endeavor to be in it more often?

- **Intense concentration:** Being in the flow leads to higher quality and quantity work.
- **Enhanced clarity:** The body and mind know what needs to be done without having to think about it. It's like operating automatically from your higher abilities.
- **No doubts or obstacles:** Feelings of stress, worry, and self-doubt take a back seat in the flow state.
- **The feel-good factor:** Being in flow is an intrinsically positive experience, a pleasure that comes with being in the moment and doing something you love.
- **Lasting fulfillment:** The happiness created by being in the flow fosters a general sense of well-being, happiness, and fulfillment.
- **Accessing the "super-self":** In this state, your higher cognitive and physical abilities become activated, turbo-charging performance, creativity, problem-solving, and mental processes; in short, you tap into the better part, version, or aspect of yourself.

  Csikszentmihalyi interviewed many high-performing individuals from diverse and challenging professions. They all emphasized the importance of the flow state. His research has helped identify what is required to get in the flow. The next page has a few suggestions.

Hack 10: The Fundamentals:

The following conditions are prerequisites to the flow state:

- **Acting on your passion:** You can only reach a flow state when you are doing something you genuinely enjoy.
- **Acting on your talents:** The activity should also be something you are good at and in alignment with who you are.
- **Just challenging enough:** The task should not be overly easy or difficult. It should present a challenge but be well within your capabilities.
- **Focusing on the journey, not the result:** To borrow another example from sport, this can be described as a runner concentrating on his race and not the gold medal.

Hack 11: How to Get in The Flow?

The following things can help you reach this state regularly:

- **No distractions:** Eliminate as many of the things that disturb and distract you as possible. Find a quiet place to work, put your phone away, try a website blocker, etc.
- **Create a ritual:** A meditation, a short walk, a pot of tea, or music can help calm the so-called "monkey mind" and put you in the mood. These rituals condition your mind to prepare for that state. The more you do it, the easier it gets.
- **Keep a journal:** Observing conditions and recording your responses is especially helpful when learning to get in the flow. Begin by identifying the times when your mind most naturally functions at full speed. Note the changes to your ritual and their respective results. Ask questions like, "Does music distract me or get me in the mood? Do I think more clearly on a full or an empty stomach?" UFC fighter Micahel Chandler maintains a journal after each training session when he reaches the flow state, looking for things he could repeat daily.
- **Mono-task the most important assignment:** The flow state is reached while focusing on something that requires significant brainpower. Multitasking creates distractions, which make it impossible to get into the flow. Focus on the day's main task during your most productive time.

"What you think you become.
What you feel you attract.
What you imagine you create."
- Buddha

6

USING THE LAW OF ATTRACTION

"Whatever you hold in your mind on a consistent basis is exactly what you will experience in your life." – Tony Robbin

Losing yourself doing something you love is referred to as being in a flow state of mind; "being in the vortex" is how Abraham-Hicks's books on the Law of Attraction (LOA) describe a flow state of *life* when wishes become a reality effortlessly. Since we chalk that up to luck, something we cannot control, we are left feeling powerless, even envious of the few who are blessed with good fortune. The great news is that there is no such thing as luck; everyone can get into the flow state of life.

Whether they know how they are doing it or not, lucky people create fortuitous circumstances in the "manifestation vortex" by using the LOA effectively.

The vortex is a non-physical realm that holds all your desires. To 'enter' it, you need to adjust your vibration (i.e., your thoughts and feelings) enough to experience the things you want, like changing programs on a TV set. "It is unlimited what the universe can bring when you understand the great secret, that thoughts become things," author Fearless Soul writes.

Understanding the Law of Attraction

From the Buddha to Napoleon Hill to *The Secret* and beyond, the material explaining this universal law is staggering. The basic definition is that energy is attracted to the energy of the same resonance, or simply "like attracts like." Thoughts and feelings are energy, so when we focus on something, corresponding experiences manifest in our lives; our thoughts/feelings become a reality.

For example, if you constantly worry about getting sick, you will probably keep getting sick. It's important to understand that the LOA does not know or care if something is good or bad for you. It functions as a mirror, reflecting what you are thinking/feeling exactly in the form of external circumstances. Or think of it as an internet search: the universal bots and algorithms serve up content based on your keywords and interests. So, if you don't like the results, adjust the search parameters.

Simple as that sounds, it is not easy. We, humans, are highly emotional beings with little or no control over our thoughts. The law is immutable: it delivers precisely what you ordered every time, regardless of whether you enjoy the package or not. "Why would I ever want to make myself sick?" you might protest. Well, it's not about what you want but what you focus on consciously and subconsciously most of the time. For example, if you obsess about your health or if people in your environment are passing on their fear of illness to you. Some may dismiss this as superstitious mumbo-jumbo; the reality is that unless you learn to use the LOA to your benefit – because it is an uncompromising double-edged sword – thriving becomes difficult, if not impossible.

Using the Law of Attraction

There is no bypassing or fooling the LOA. You can use it to shape the life you desire or let it be created randomly. The greatest problem people face, and understandably so, is that external circumstances trigger their feelings and thoughts. They are carried hither and thither in a sea of emotions, which generate erratic manifestations.

To manifest things you prefer, you need to hold matching thoughts, feelings, and intent long enough for them to become real. If you want better experiences tomorrow, you must have better-feeling thoughts today. When you wait to feel good when something good happens, you put the proverbial cart before the horse – that's like rubbing your reflection in the mirror trying to wipe the dirt off your face.

You need to feel good before good things happen; you need to believe something before you see it in your reality, not wait to see it to believe it – this is the crux of the LAO.

Since most people do not operate this way, they keep manifesting things they do not want. You can change this by shifting your default negative mindsets and self-talk. As Robin Sharma says, you see the world not as it is but as you are.

Don't focus on problems but opportunities; don't focus on what you hate but on what you love; don't see yourself as a victim of circumstance but as the one who controls their future. The LOA is more than positive thinking; it is the only way to navigate life successfully.

Hack 12: Manifestation Practices and Tools:

Although this is not an exhaustive list, the following suggestions will help you use the LOA more effectively:

- **Daydreams, visualizations:** When you decide what you want to attract into your reality, imagine the desired outcome in detail and often. Make-believe that it has already manifested feeling those emotions as genuinely and as long as possible.
- **Affirmations, hypnosis:** Our mindsets start being programmed into our subconscious minds in childhood. If your parents were always saying, "We don't have enough," lacking becomes your default. By repeating an affirmation like, "I have enough," you overwrite the default program, actually creating new neuropathways in your brain. Hypnosis speeds up the process.
- **Phrasing:** The affirmation "I will be rich someday" defers the manifestation to the future. Rephrasing it to "I am rich" or "How did I get rich so quickly?" instructs the universe to create that reality as soon as possible. Also, the LOA registers negative statements like "I don't want to be poor" as "poor," reinforcing the very thing that you don't want because you are focused on the fear of poverty, not the joy of prosperity.
- **Thought-control:** When you have a problem, work on solutions without fixating on negative scenarios. Do not hold onto the energy of the problem in your "creation vortex" by thinking about it constantly. Say, "No, I will not think about that," and distract yourself with something positive when fearful thoughts come.
- **Resistance:** Often, even when we do all the right things, the manifestation fails – this indicates that resistance is keeping us in a negative vibration.

If you keep visualizing your dream home but subconsciously feel that you are not worthy of such luxury, your true feelings will thwart the manifestation. Since everything you resist persists, you need to locate and clear any underlying resistance. Try soul-searching through journaling, psychoanalysis, guided meditation, or conversation with a trusted friend.

Hack 13: Raising Your Vibration:

The LAO responds to how you feel more powerfully, quickly, and efficiently than your thoughts and words, and it cannot be fooled. If you say, "I feel confident," when you are fearful, the manifestation will match your feelings, not your words.

So, the key is managing your emotions and raising your vibration. How? Deliberately and gradually. For example, do not suppress your fear; it is perfectly natural and needs to be expressed. Suppressing it will only create resistance.

Give yourself some time to feel uneasy but do not wallow in it. As soon as possible, reach for a better feeling by playing with your pet, for example. By engaging in joyful activities and thoughts, you can deliberately raise your vibration bit by bit, moving from feelings of limitation to empowerment.

According to the Abraham-Hicks teachings, the scale from the lowest to the highest emotional resonance is as follows:

- Fear-despair-grief-depression
- Guilt-unworthiness; hatred-rage
- Revenge
- Anger
- Worry
- Frustration
- Contentment
- Optimism
- Enthusiasm
- Love-joy-gratitude.

7

CULTIVATING THE ABUNDANT MINDSET

"See yourself living in abundance, and you will attract it. It always works; it works every time, with every person." - Bob Proctor.

One of the most critical internal shifts one needs to thrive is clearing the myth of lack and scarcity. If you are operating from this perspective, you inadvertently create that reality through the Law of Attraction. When you buy into this false myth, you feel like a victim of external circumstances and allow yourself to be manipulated. Mainstream media endlessly broadcasts doom and gloom, generating helplessness, pessimism, negativity, and – in turn – depression, anxiety, and fear. It takes advantage of the role "amygdala" (a small almond-sized part of the brain behind the ears) that constantly scans the environment for threats.

While it served its purpose when hunter-gatherers had to contend with wild animals, times are different now. Doomsday narratives keep us tuned in so that advertisers will keep paying for "eyeballs," as viewers are often termed, making full use of this 'feature' in our brain.

For example, often referred to as "Constant Negative News" or the "Crisis News Network," CNN gained traction during the Gulf War for the copious negative and gory information it broadcasted.

It's important to understand that these networks are paid to brainwash the population on the agenda "du-jour" to drive up stock and food prices, sell pharmaceuticals, and convince voters to support wars based on fear mongering. They manufacture unwitting consent by keeping people in a constant flight-or-fight mode, which is not conducive to creativity, the pursuit of excellence, and critical thinking.

A recent example was "the toilet paper crisis" during the first few weeks of the pandemic in 2020. The media created an artificial shortage because people were stocking ridiculous amounts of tissue and trying to profiteer.

The Age of Abundance:

To help reframe our perspective, let's take a closer look at the meaning of abundance. The dictionary defines it as the state or condition of having a copious quantity of something; plentifulness of the good things in life; prosperity. As you can see, it does not refer only to money. So, the first thing we need to do is broaden our understanding. You may not have wealth, but you do have great health and vitality.

You have plentiful choices when it comes to education, career, and where you want to live. The internet puts endless resources and information at your fingertips, blowing open the doors of innovation. Nature is the utmost expression of abundance, and so are its gifts, like healing herbs, nutritious food, and beauty. Contrary to popular belief, I'm here to tell you that we are living in the Golden Age. Technological advances are bringing about significant change and enabling everyone to thrive.

> *"There is a lie that acts like a virus within the mind of humanity. And that lie is, 'There's not enough good to go around. There's lack and there's limitation and there's just not enough.'*
> *The truth is that there's more than enough good to go around. There are more than enough creative ideas. There is more than enough power. There is more than enough love. There's more than enough joy.*
> *All of this begins to come through a mind that is aware of its own infinite nature. There is enough for everyone. If you believe it, if you can see it, if you act from it, it will show up for you. That's the truth."*
> *- Michael Beckwith*

Here are a few examples:

- The average life expectancy has increased from 31 to 72.6 years since 1900. According to Ray Kurzweil, "By 2022, medical technology will be more than a thousand times more advanced than it is today, [...] with every new year of research guaranteeing at least one more year of life expectancy." This has become a distinct possibility due to the exponential advancements in cellular biology, artificial intelligence, and robotics (nanobots, to be specific). According to Cambridge scientist Aubrey de Grey, the first immortal humans have already been born.

- Mobiles are increasing connectivity and functionality by the day. According to Statistica, approximately 4.57 billion people were active users of the Internet in April 2020. This rapidly-increasing number represents 59% of the global population. Information is education, power, and self-empowerment.
- 3D Printing is making things faster and cheaper. The construction industry is no exception. Imagine building a house in a few days using large 3D printers!
- Shared economies like Uber and Airbnb have simplified life for more people and provided additional income for millions.
- The cost of energy is falling so fast that Ray Kurzweil thinks that the cost of electricity will trend to zero by 2040. Moreover, the price of solar panels has dropped exponentially. Think of the possibilities of free energy! Cheaper and cleaner fuel (solar) will give rise to increased electric and autonomous cars.
- According to RethinkX, "By 2030, 95% of U.S. passenger miles traveled will be served by on-demand autonomous electric vehicles owned by fleets, not individuals, in a new business model called "Transport-as-a-service" (TaaS). RethinkX suggests that TaaS disruption will have an enormous impact on the existing transportation and oil industries but create trillions in new business opportunities, consumer surplus, and GDP growth.
- Extensive research is being conducted to eradicate air and water pollution, thereby creating a better environment.

Without a doubt, such advancements will help uplift humanity and all life on the planet. We are in the Golden Age, which Peter Diamandis from Singularity University simply calls "abundance." I do not deny that we have significant challenges. Hunger, lack of access to clean water, and education are still affecting too many.

The pollution of the oceans and the destruction of the rainforests also need to be addressed urgently. We need to think about food security for an ever-growing global population and make cities more human-friendly living spaces. However, solutions exist for most – if not all – of these problems already.

Dedicated individuals are making strides, like Boyan Slat, who is working on cleaning the oceans, and Scott Harrison, whose goal is to ensure that every human being has access to clean drinking water. Countless permaculture and urban green initiatives are showing us how we can grow enough food for everyone. And the list goes on and on. The challenge is to give these initiatives enough support and exposure so they can succeed.

That's where every one of us can contribute. When we live our lives with purpose, we make choices aligned with our values. Every time we buy something, we cast a vote. Every time we eat something, we make a choice. Every time we apply for a job, we show our alliances.

Just like the big vision for our life is important, our small everyday choices matter too. We all have the power to be the change we want to see in the world. Having the knowledge and confidence that we can bring forth massive change, let's make the best use of our time on this planet!

However, we cannot move forward into a bright future if we are stuck in a lack and scarcity mindset collectively and individually. Here are a few suggestions to help you develop a mindset of abundance:

Hack 14: Program Your Subconscious:

- **Stop the negative programming:** Mainstream media is one of the biggest sources of stress in our daily lives. It may not appear that way because we are so used to listening to the prophets of doom 24/7, but you will feel the difference when you disconnect from their constant poisoning. Also, limit the time you spend with pessimistic people because they inadvertently reinforce the programming you aim to break.

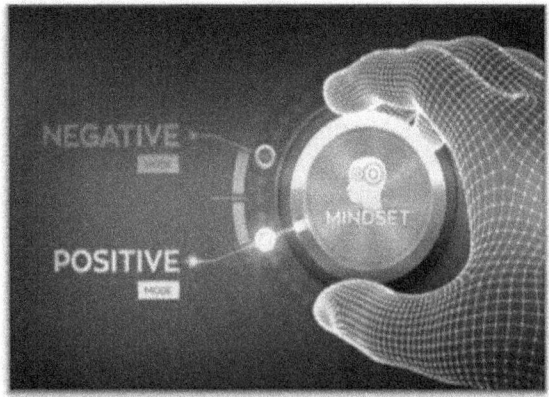

- **Begin the positive programming:** Use affirmations to program your subconscious for abundance – this works only by repetition, meaning changing your self-talk from negative to positive.
  For example, instead of thinking, "I don't have enough money," keep telling yourself, "I am earning more and more every day."
  To speed up the process, consider using recorded abundance affirmations (while you sleep, for example) to imprint new thought patterns in your mind. At the same time, form friendships with people with a positive outlook.

Hack 15: Manifest Through Intention, Not by Default:

The Law of Attraction says that what you think about becomes your reality. When our thoughts are focused on what we don't have, we manifest lack by default because life is a reflection of what we think about, like "a self-fulfilling prophecy." The key is to manifest consciously through intention and acting accordingly.

Hack 16: Look to the Future:

Become inspired by people who spread hope based on real science and projections, like the futurists. The ones I follow closely are:

- Ray Kurtzweil is one of the leading futurists of our time. More than 80% of his predictions have come true on or ahead of his predicted date. At present, his most prominent prediction is, "By 2029, computers will have human-level intelligence."
- Peter Diamandis, a co-founder of Singularity University with Ray Kurtzweil, is a visionary interested in space exploration. One of his recent predictions is that by 2025, the IoE will exceed 100 billion connected devices, each with a dozen or more sensors collecting data.
- Thomas Frey's predictions include, "By 2030, the average person in the U.S. will have 4.5 packages a week delivered with flying drones. They will travel 40% of the time in a driverless car, use a 3D printer to print hyper-individualized meals, and will spend most of their leisure time on an activity that hasn't been invented yet."
- Dave Asprey is more of a bio-hacker, aiming to live to 180 through various methods, many of which are already being adopted by millions.

"When you are living the best version of yourself, you inspire others to live the best versions of themselves."
- Steve Maraboli

BE YOUR BEST SELF

Harness the power of your inner soul and bring out
the best version of yourself

"Your greatest responsibility in your life is to be the best version of yourself. When you feel for what the soul believes that is who you become."
- Shannon L Alder

8

BEING AN IDEA MACHINE

"There is one thing stronger than all the armies in the world, and that is an idea whose time has come."
– Victor Hugo

Ideas are messages and urgings from our subconscious and superconscious mind to live in alignment with our life purpose. They are one way that the Law of Attraction delivers the things we desire. Ideas create opportunities and solve problems.

Without them, we would still be living in prehistoric times. No matter how simple or small, they have the potential to make a massive difference in our lives personally and collectively. They plant the seeds of how we can become our best selves, so we want to have them in abundance.

How to Become an Idea Machine?

Humans have an insatiable need to grow. When we stagnate in routines, we lose our zest for life – that's when ideas come to the rescue because they motivate us into exciting action. As James Altucher writes in his blog, you need to become an idea machine. In any meeting you attend, you need to have at least one idea ready. It must just come to you.

If a friend tells you a problem, you must be able to offer a solution in a few minutes – this may feel like a herculean task, but it isn't. It becomes relatively easy when you exercise your idea muscle regularly.

The key is to create a flow of ideas by consistently thinking about the changes you wish to make in various areas of your life and writing them down. The more ideas you generate, the higher the chances of coming up with a good one.

Coming up with good ideas takes effort, like everything else, but the pointers below will help:

- **Read and observe more:** To become an idea machine, you need to read as much as you can and observe everything. These two practices will expand your knowledge base so you can come up with relevant ideas.
- **Look for problems:** Of course, this does not mean being negative; it's actually quite the opposite. When you identify a problem through observation, you are more likely to come up with solutions. Ideas are the foundation of all entrepreneurial endeavors and inventions.
- **One idea a day:** You can start simply by writing down at least one idea a day for the following areas in your life: health, career, joy, personal finance, and self-improvement.
- **Make your brain sweat:** After you have practiced the one-idea-a-day method for some time, push yourself to write at least ten ideas every time. If it is challenging to come up with ten, try putting down twenty! The key is to get your brain to work. When performed consistently, this mind training will turn you into an idea machine.
- **There is no such thing as a bad idea:** It's a numbers game. Yes, a few ideas may not work out, and that's why it is crucial to have options. The key is to have ten ideas, of which nine may fail, but you only need one to change the world.
- **Act fast and fail quickly:** Even the best idea in the world means nothing if it's not implemented. Test your ideas, be patient, but act quickly. If left too long, they may become irrelevant, or you may lose motivation. If an idea doesn't work out, first try to fix it or find a different approach. However, you should know when to stop and embrace failure because that creates space for innovation.

- **Go with the flow:** Some of us come up with our best ideas while walking the dog or taking a shower – that's because our minds are more relaxed. We connect better to our intuition and inner sense of knowing.
- **Catalog, track, and improve:** Keep a record of all your ideas. Don't dismiss anything – what may be impossible today may be "on the leading edge of innovation" in two years. When you have a good idea, keep a record of everything you have done to implement it. Track your successes and failures in detail because they will help you see the way forward. Also, as you come up with other related ideas, you can determine how these can improve the one you are developing.
- **Don't be the "idea guy":** You know, the one who discusses his ideas with practically everyone but never executes them.

There are several issues when you become that guy:

- You become annoying, and if you're unable to follow through, you lose credibility.
- You're also likely to lose motivation after talking to many people. Not everyone will understand your idea, so it may be shot down or, worse, stolen.

Below are a few hacks to help you collect and organize your ideas, which can potentially change the world:

Hack 17: Use Tools, and Keep Them Handy:

Ideas and thoughts are mercurial, here one moment, gone the next. Unless you write them down quickly, they will slip away. Make use of the following tools and methods:

- **Create an idea journal:** Buy a small notebook and jot down your ideas immediately. I prefer a notebook to an app because we remember better when we write things down.
  Keep a waterproof pad and pen handy if you have ideas in the shower. If you come up with ideas just before bed, keep your journal on your nightstand.
- **Anywhere, anytime:** How many times have we heard about people jotting down brilliant ideas on a napkin at a coffee shop? The rule of thumb is, scribble it down on anything, anywhere, immediately. Don't wait until you get home.

- **Use apps:** If you're glued to your phone, you may prefer curating your ideas using apps like Evernote or Google Notes, which can be linked to your calendar.

Here's a list of other excellent tools:

- **Milanotes:** It is a free and easy-to-use tool that enables you to compile complex ideas. It lets you post images and links. It's perfect if you're a writer and need to keep all your ideas in one place. You can create vision boards, too.
- **Diaro:** It is like an online journal where you can put down your thoughts.
- **Trello:** It is a great tool to list your tasks and ideas. You can also create groups to brainstorm.
- **Feedly:** A lot like Pinterest, it helps you compile all your articles in one place. It has an easy interface. You can even save the items to revisit them later. Tools like this spark new ideas because you will be reading so much about the topic.
- **Slack** and **Simple Mind:** These are great tools if you're the brainstorming kind. The former also helps you collaborate with colleagues. You and your team can bounce ideas off each other. The latter works more like a mind map; it connects your ideas. It's helpful for visual learners and aids comprehension.

9

BEING PRODUCTIVE

"Don't count the days. Make the days count."
-Muhammad Ali

The advice, "Don't be the idea guy," points to the need to balance thought and imagination with action. To thrive, you need to be both an idea machine and a productivity engine. Today, productivity is a buzzword, grossly misunderstood as being busy and working to the point of burnout. Let's begin by grasping the concept before learning how to put it into practice. In economics, productivity measures the output per unit input, such as labor or capital. An employee is considered productive when their work yields high profits and significant results.

James Clear interprets it as the measure of a person's efficiency in completing a task. Productivity is often misunderstood as getting more things done when, in fact, it is about getting the important things done consistently. It is about maintaining an average speed on a few essential things and not maximum speed on all items.

> **That said, there is no one-size-fits-all template.
> Your productivity plan will be
> unique to your workday and goals.**

The Benefits of Productivity:

Why can't we do the bare minimum and get on with life? Unfortunately, that's how it is for most people, yet human beings have extraordinary potential. We must use our time on this planet well.

Here are some of the benefits of being productive:

- **Mood upliftment, happiness:** We derive satisfaction from creating something worthwhile or completing a task well. We feel that our efforts have improved the quality of our lives and the lives of others – this can be as simple as cleaning the house to enjoy a nicer environment.
- **Purpose:** Being productive helps you set and reach goals. It can be addictive because it gives you a sense of purpose and accomplishment. It adds value to your life.
- **Motivation, inspiration:** When you see the fruits of your labor, you are motivated to continue. At the same time, you motivate and inspire others to do better – this applies to all areas of life, family, workplace, and beyond.
- **Growth, innovation:** Productive people are more likely to develop their skills and learn faster. Because they serve as role models, they spark change in others. Increased productivity leads to new ideas, innovation, and progress.

How to Increase Your Productivity?

Assuming that my arguments in favor of productivity have convinced you, let me show you how to achieve it. James Clear shares the following strategies:

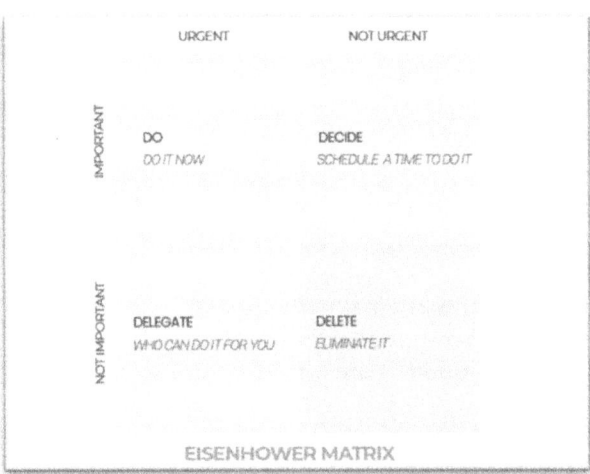

- **The Eisenhower Box:** The rule of thumb is to work smarter, not harder, and do more in less time. To do that, you must strategize. Create a matrix like the one shown above to help organize your tasks and take action.

- **The two-list strategy**: Warren Buffet proposed prioritizing tasks using the process of elimination. Start by writing down the 25 most important goals/tasks on a paper named List B. Then circle the five highest-priority tasks/goals. Put those on a new sheet as List A. Begin working on the essentials right away.
- **The Ivy Lee method:** This approach is straightforward, easy to implement, and yields excellent results. All you have to do is start and finish the most important task first thing each day.
- **To-do lists:** Make a to-do list and check off items. If you feel you need a head start every morning, create a list for the following day before leaving work – this means your tasks are already defined. All you have to do is act upon them.
- **Accountability partner:** Putting things off or fearing them is the most significant cause of unproductivity. If you struggle with procrastination, get an accountability partner who will praise you when you complete a task on time and be disappointed when you don't.
- **The Pareto Principle:** Economist Vilfredo Pareto argues that it takes only 20% of the effort to produce 80% of the results in most situations. You can implement the Pareto Principle by putting 20% of quality effort into doing a task well.

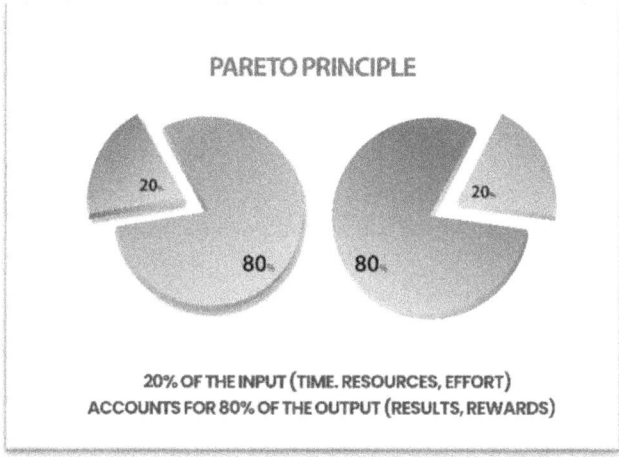

If you have ten jobs to complete, choose the two that will have the most impact and allocate your energy and time to them first.
- **The Pomodoro Technique:** This popular method is easy to implement and provides excellent results. Here, you set a timer to 25 minutes and begin a task. After 25 minutes, take a break for five minutes – this is termed "the Pomodoro session." Sessions like these help reduce procrastination.

- **Deep work:** Put forward by Cal Newport, this method is ideal for cognitively demanding tasks and mastering skills quickly. It entails focusing entirely on an assignment without distractions. You give 100% to finishing the job or learning.
- **Monotasking.** The human brain is not designed for multitasking. Research shows that doing too many things at once reduces productivity by 40%. For example, focus solely on writing your blog. Don't type away while explaining how to download photos to someone on the phone.

The following story by Robin Sharma illustrates that mastery requires productivity, which is attained by monotasking.

> *Years ago, there was a sword-crafter who was known worldwide for his work. One day, the king said, 'I must meet this man,' so his people found him in a tiny village and brought him to the king. The sword-crafter was very humble and gentle. The king was gracious and welcoming. Then the king asked, 'What is the secret to your extraordinary excellence?' The sword-crafter replied, 'Well, it's elementary, my king. Ever since I was a child, I was exposed to the craft of making swords. I fell in love with it. It didn't only speak to my head and my logic. It spoke to me at the deepest, most soulful level. It spoke to my heart. I made a decision that I would be the master sword-crafter.' He continued, 'As I grew up, I read books on sword-crafting, and if something did not relate to sword-crafting, I did not spend my time with it. That is the secret of my mastery.'*

Contrary to popular belief, productivity is simple. As all the above methods indicate, all it takes is organization to be efficient. Armed with the tips and knowledge mentioned above, you are sure to thrive if you implement what works for you. Below are a few additional hacks to help you:

Hack 18: Use Productivity Tools:

Tools like RescueTime or a simple timer can stop you from losing track of time, over-committing, or under-committing to a task.

Hack 19: Say 'NO':

People often think that they are more productive when they fill their day with all kinds of things. What ends up happening is that they are overwhelmed, and the work is of low quality. Don't take on more than you can handle. Say 'no' to things that are unimportant or demand too much from you. You may want to seize every opportunity, but make sure that it's aligned with your goals.

Hack 20: Rise Early:

Everyone is always complaining that there aren't enough hours in the day. Why not add a couple? Early birds catch the worm. For instance, wake up at 6 am, spend time journaling, reading, and making to-do lists before starting your day. Do this for a month and see the difference in your productivity levels.

Hack 21: Use Your Commute:

If you travel to work, or anywhere for that matter, use it by listening to podcasts or audiobooks. You will learn a great deal, from improved vocabulary to new ideas. You can also make important calls to save time.

Hack 22: Social Media Detox:

On average, people spend more than two hours on social media sites like Twitter and Instagram. Limit the use of these apps. Spend that time reading a book or watching an informative documentary.

Hack 23: Automate, Delegate, and Eliminate:

- Look for faster ways of completing tasks without compromising quality.
- Speed up tasks using software. For example, use Grammarly to check spelling and grammar in your documents.
- Delegate. For instance, give a trusted colleague the task of fact-checking a presentation rather than doing it yourself.
- Eliminate time-consuming tasks and redundant communication. For example, rather than traveling across town for a follow-up meeting that does not require your physical presence, do it via Zoom or a phone call. Reduce the number of items to be discussed in meetings to crucial ones. Eliminate fluff; keep your communications as precise and brief as possible.

"If you have integrity, nothing else matters. If you don't have integrity, nothing else matters."
-Alan Simpson

10

INTEGRITY IS THE WAY OF LIFE

"Real integrity is doing the right thing, knowing that nobody's going to know whether you did it or not."
- Oprah Winfrey

The dictionary defines integrity as the quality of possessing and steadfastly adhering to high moral principles or professional standards. One is thought to have integrity when one is honest consistently. To my mind, it also means keeping your word irrespective of the challenges – this goes hand in hand with productivity. For instance, if you promise to complete a task within a stipulated time and quality, you fulfill the promise without compromising any aspect despite any hurdles you may encounter. Author Spencer Johnson defines integrity as telling the truth to ourselves.

"Integrity is telling myself the truth. And honesty is telling the truth to other people."
— Spencer Johnson

His definition differentiates integrity and honesty, which is merely telling the truth to other people. In simple terms, integrity also means being true to yourself, being authentic. When we consider the above definitions, we see that many people fall short on certain aspects. As a result, they rate low on the "trustworthiness meter," meaning that other people do not necessarily have confidence in them.

Trust is earned through consistent integrity. Whether friends or professionals, people of high integrity are greatly valued. As they present the best versions of themselves and deliver on their promises every time, they are offered excellent opportunities at work and in life. Integrity is, therefore, a crucial trait that we all need to have if we want to thrive.

How to Cultivate Integrity:

No, you are not born with it! While it is true that some people are naturally more honest and trustworthy, integrity can be developed. As such, it is not effortless. The following suggestions will help:

- Always present your best self. How? By acting on your highest potential in all your interactions. Start with the basics, like keeping yourself and your environment clean – this shows that you take yourself seriously and have high self-worth. Mind your manners and adhere to social norms, like being on time. If you are consistently late for appointments, how can anyone entrust you with a task or an opportunity?
- Keep improving yourself by completing personal projects, learning new things, etc. This expands your scope and inspires confidence in others.
- Keep your promises. To be a person of integrity, one must keep their promises and oaths. Conflict and disappointment arise when a person does not deliver. Therefore, people value those who consistently deliver. Never go back on your word, stick to deadlines, produce quality work, etc. People must have a reason to trust you.
- Never lie. Be honest in all your communications, even if that means that people may be disappointed. For example, if you can't do a job within the allocated timeframe, turn it down. This ensures that you don't overcommit and enables you to provide clarity in all your personal and professional relationships. If you're unable to deliver something due to unforeseen circumstances, speak to those concerned. They will surely understand, and you can work it out from there.

Bobby Jones was a golf player who played national and international matches approximately one century ago. He was famous for his honesty and sportsmanship. In the U.S. Open in Boston, 1925, he hit his ball on the 11th hole.
He insisted that he had moved the ball slightly by accidentally clipping the grass. He told the officials that he had violated Rule 18 (moving the ball), but they didn't agree. He stayed firm, and they finally had to accept.
He lost the game by the same margin, one stroke. The sportswriters praised him for his honesty, to which he replied, "You might as well praise me for not robbing banks."

The takeaway from this story is that integrity is not always easy or satisfying. At times, you may end up with losses but earn respect from your peers and yourself.

While integrity is a noble and required trait for thriving, it should not be at the expense of your physical and mental health. In the name of integrity, people spread themselves too thin. Have clear boundaries as to what you can and will do. Communicate these boundaries honestly and politely. Integrity is a core value usually developed in early childhood through observation and repetition. It is crucial to raise children in an environment conducive to ethical values. That said, today is a great time to learn and adopt something noble.

Here are a few hacks to help you:

Hack 24: The Integrity Checklist:

Integrity is doing the right thing, even when no one is watching.
- C. S. Lewis

In an article about success, Robin Amster lists the following steps to cultivating integrity:

- Fulfill your promises and keep all appointments.
- Think carefully before making a commitment. Be realistic about your promises.
- Say "no," and be comfortable with it. You can't do it all, and that's OK. Always introspect and examine your knee-jerk reactions. What are they signaling?
- Work on fixing your malicious behavior and poor manners. Develop effective and confident communication to avoid misunderstandings.
- Avoid people who lack integrity.

Hack 25: Say What You Mean, Do What You Say:

If you are unsure whether you can keep your word, it's always best to admit it upfront. Never allow yourself to think that you can refuse to do what you have promised. Be honest and clear from the start. Avoid sugarcoating feedback or opinions. Be precise and straightforward.

Hack 26: Be Accountable:

There may be occasions when you mess up. You may not be able to go through with something because of a mistake or an emergency. Take responsibility in times like these. Offer to clean up the mess. Accountability is crucial at all times on both personal and professional fronts.

Hack 27: Surround Yourself with People Who Value and Practice Integrity:

We are defined by the company we keep because our friends have a big influence on our lives. To cultivate integrity, socialize with people who have this trait. Avoid mindless gossip and indulge in healthy, meaningful conversations.

Hack 28: Focus on The Small Things; The Larger Ones Will Sort Themselves Out:

By focusing on the small but significant things that you can control, you can cultivate integrity. For instance, if you want your team to perform well in a project, instead of worrying and whining, do your part well. Then you can rest assured that you've done the right thing. Even if the project does not meet the ideal standard, your effort will be seen and valued.

11

MASTERING YOUR HABITS

*"Your beliefs become your thoughts,
Your thoughts become your words,
Your words become your actions,
Your actions become your habits,
Your habits become your values,
Your values become your destiny."*
- Gandhi

Predominant behavior learned from our surroundings is formed by the age of seven. Since 95% of our daily activities are routine-based, they are controlled by our subconscious mind, making us truly the creatures of habit, good and bad. If unchecked, habits can create dependencies and turn into addictions. For example, drinking every night after work to unwind may lead to alcoholism. To make sure we understand the difference, let's look at the following definitions:

Habit (n.) A settled tendency or usual manner of behavior. An acquired mode of behavior that has become nearly or completely involuntary.
Addiction (n.) A behavior pattern acquired by frequent repetition or physiologic exposure that shows itself in regularity or increased facility of performance.

While addiction is always detrimental, we can truly thrive when we gain mastery of our habits, breaking the non-beneficial or destructive and intentionally adopting the beneficial. Approximately 43% of our daily behaviors are performed habitually, based on patterns imprinted on our neural pathways.

So, it's a question of reprogramming ourselves by understanding how the mind works, conscious and subconscious.

The former takes care of awareness, helping us form thoughts and make decisions. The latter functions like a tape recorder. It doesn't know what's ethical or unethical, beneficial or detrimental; it simply does what it has been taught.

How to Identify Bad Habits?

Before you can create good habits, you must identify and break the detrimental ones. Begin by taking inventory of a typical day from the moment you wake up until you go to sleep. Consider a habit useful if it contributes positively to your life and bad if it is detrimental.

When you identify bad habits, like spending too much money on frivolous things, examine the underlying forces that cause the habit to perpetuate. Think about when, how, and why it formed. What circumstances are maintaining it now? Is it truly a habit or an addiction? If you identify something that is an addiction or bordering on one, seek professional help – the sooner, the better.

The next step is to think about your life. Are you in a good place? Your successes or failures are mostly the results of subconscious programming. If you're not happy, eliminate unhealthy habits like the following:

- **Procrastination:** This means putting off doing something against your better judgment – that's why psychologists often connect procrastination to self-harm. It's not laziness. We procrastinate because we fear failure or are averse to the task. Tuning into your body will help identify whether the procrastination is due to anxiety or fear.
  If it is, you can soothe yourself (e.g., make your favorite tea as you begin the dreaded task) or reward yourself when you complete it. You cannot simply wish procrastination away; it must be dealt with consciously using intention and willpower. Break down the task into smaller parts, and work on them one at a time. Brian Tracey's advice is to "eat the frog first," tackling the most dreaded task first thing in the day.
- **Expecting immediate results:** This is essentially the inability to delay gratification. Research shows that individuals who delay gratification do better in life than those who don't, as demonstrated by Walter Mischel's Stanford marshmallow experiment (circa 1972). A group of 32 kids was given candy and asked not to eat it if they wanted another later. Thirty years later, the kids who had delayed gratification were successful adults.

Those who didn't were not as successful. Why? Few remain committed to goals because they cannot delay gratification, like having the willpower to invest their money rather than buy a luxury car.

- **Limiting beliefs; negative self-talk:** Many of us hold deeply ingrained beliefs about ourselves that are not correct; in fact, they are self-destructive. Psychiatrists call this "the little mean myth" that we are not smart or worthy enough. We are always telling bad stories about ourselves, and eventually, we end up unconsciously doing things to make those stories come true; we self-sabotage.
  Statements like, "I am not talented, intelligent, or attractive enough" lead to insecurity and depression. Eliminating negative self-talk is key if you want to thrive. Don't beat yourself up for mistakes and bad choices. Focus on the positive. Let go of old stories and ideas that weigh you down.
- **Self-perception:** You can re-calibrate and improve your self-perception with these four elements given by confidence-researcher Don Moore: Measure your ability, talk to others, be practical, and think in shades of gray. Once you begin to realize how competent you are and accomplish something worthwhile, you will become more confident. You will find value in yourself, and your self-perception will improve.
- **Scarcity mindset:** Instead of seeing abundance all around, we focus on what we don't have and worry about what we might lose. This mindset leads to anxiety, stress, jealousy, and in few cases, isolation. Ultimately, the scarcity mindset is a vicious cycle of misery and limiting beliefs that keep feeding each other. To break the pattern, you need to shift your perspective. Focus on the things you are grateful for, embrace the abundance mindset, and make it a habit.

How to Change Your Habits?

To change your habits, you must reprogram your subconscious mind, using modalities like hypnotherapy, Psych-K programming, and the following suggestions:

- **Self-control:** The first step is to shift your thoughts from negative to positive. **Studies show:** To convert harmful habits to productive ones, you must exercise self-control. You need to monitor your habitual behavior.
  A reasonable level of self-control leads to better long-term outcomes. Mindfulness and meditation help a great deal in teaching self-control.

- **Repetition:** To form a new habit, follow actions consistently. When you start an exercise regimen, you will find that the second day is much harder than the thirtieth. This is because the feelings of reluctance and resistance shrink away with time.

To form a new habit, follow the following steps:

- Identify the change you need to make in yourself
- Create a list of goal-based actions, and
- Begin implementing the activities every day.

Ensure that the activities are process-oriented (e.g., walking for 20 minutes instead of losing a few pounds a month). Such actions provide better positive reinforcement because you can control them.

Studies show that a goal can be more powerful when linked to a concrete trigger, reminding us to engage in a positive habit. For instance, every time you crave chocolate, grab a fruit instead.

The key is to make healthier choices.

James Clear, the author of Atomic Habits, offers the following suggestions:

- Establish cues to remind you of the habit you need to cultivate, like pairing the new pattern with an old one; for example, working out immediately after brushing your teeth in the morning.
- Create an environment that is conducive to your new habit. If you have resolved to eat healthily, don't keep candy on your desk.
- Make it attractive for yourself by pairing what you want to do with what you need to do. Watch your favorite series as you walk on the treadmill.
- Keep it easy but consistent. For example, commit to exercising 30 minutes every day for 30 days – this will not overwhelm you. When you have formed the habit, you can increase it to 45-60 minutes every day. **Remember, it's okay to miss a day but not two.**
- Reward yourself when you practice a healthy habit. Ensure the reward is in proportion to the effort required in maintaining the habit. While you're at it, track your patterns on a calendar or app.
- Armed with the above techniques, you can create new healthy habits. Don't fall for myths like, "It takes 21 days to form a habit." On the contrary, research has shown that it takes exactly **66 days** for a behavior to become automatic.

Here are a few hacks to help you:

Hack 29: Use the 3 Rs:

The 3 Rs of creating good habits, as given by James Clear are: remind, routine, reward. Use reminders (e.g., on your devices) to do the required action. The action needs to be done at a particular time every day, thereby making it a routine. Finally, reward yourself for the effort. After a successful week of eating healthy foods, treat yourself to a dessert on Sunday.

Hack 30: Set a Daily Routine:

Routines help you prioritize your tasks and stay focused. This is especially helpful if you tend to procrastinate.

- **You can have 2-3 daily routines:**
  o Morning routine to get the best possible start to the day; a routine after you return from work; a night routine that might include reflecting on your day.
  o Did you get the most important things done? If something wasn't done, decide whether it is still vital. If yes, schedule it for the next day.

Hack 31: It's Easier to Replace Than Eliminate:

Rather than trying to eliminate a bad habit, replace it with a good one. Select the behavior you want to change and decide what to do instead. For example, a friend who loves singing wished to stop smoking. Every time she was tempted to pick up a cigarette, she would pick up her guitar and sing.

Hack 32: Have an Accountability Partner:

Ask someone you trust and respect to hold you accountable for the changes you want to make in your life. This will add positive pressure, compelling you to stick to your commitment every day. It is also rewarding to receive positive affirmation from a friend.

"Be careful with your words. Once they are said, they can be only forgiven, not forgotten."

12

MINDING YOUR WORDS

"You are master of what you say until you utter it; once you deliver it, you are its captive. Preserve your tongue as you do your gold and money. One word could bring disgrace and the termination of a bliss."
— Ali Ibn Abi Talib A.S

Blurting things out without thinking is a terrible habit, which shows a lack of self-control, a reactionary personality, untrustworthiness, etc. To thrive professionally and personally, we must gain mastery over what we say.

Words are extremely powerful; Hitler's speeches instigated hatred and fascism, while Gandhi's made people realize the importance of peace. Edward Bulwer-Lytton said, "The pen is mightier than the sword," in 1839. Could that be more relevant than it is today when social media enables people to spew poison hidden behind the screen?

Personalities and life trajectories are shaped by words, as illustrated in the following story by former Indian President Dr. Abdul Kalam:

> *"When I was a kid, my mom cooked food for us. One night, when she had made dinner after a long hard day's work, mom placed a plate of sabzi (curry) and extremely burnt roti in front of my dad.*
> *I was waiting to see if anyone noticed the roti. But dad just ate his roti and asked me how my day was at school. I heard mom apologizing to dad for the burnt roti. And I'll never forget what he said: 'Honey, I love burnt roti.' Later that night, I went to kiss Daddy goodnight and asked him*
> *if he really liked his roti burnt.*
> *He wrapped me in his arms and said:*
> *Your momma put in a long hard day at work and was really tired. And besides... a burnt roti never hurts anyone, but harsh words do!'"*

Following his father's example, Kalam grew up to be sensible and kind-hearted. In contrast, Michael Jackson's father was cruel. He made fun of his face as a teenager, leading Michael to alter his appearance endlessly.

Albert Einstein could not talk until he was four, and his schoolmaster declared he would never amount to anything. Luckily, his parents encouraged him to be independent and creative.

The things we say to each other have a profound effect. If your mouth is a "loose cannon," or you wish to refine your communication style, consider the following suggestions:

Hack 33: How to Speak Mindfully:

These tips will help you control the tendency to speak carelessly, make you a better conversation partner and someone people want to interact with, and do wonders for your personal and professional life.

- **Know your audience:** You would not discuss quantum mechanics with a child. Understand your conversation partner and cater to their needs.
- **Put yourself in the other person's shoes:** Be mindful of the other person's situation. Don't boast about luxuries in front of someone who is struggling to make ends meet.
- **Listen:** Always respond to what the person has said; this makes for effective dialogue. Many people are in a rush to speak, wanting to control the conversation.
  However, the one who listens has the advantage because they are aware of all points made. Listen 80% of the time, and speak 20%.
- **Make people feel special:** Make a habit of acknowledging people's efforts, using positive phrases like "I'm proud of you," "You deserve this, and more."

Another way of making someone feel special is by addressing them with their names, especially in large meetings and groups.
- **Know your place:** Before making any comments, make sure that you have the right to speak about the matter and that your input was requested.
- **Stay positive:** If you are always whining, you spread negativity. Instead of telling yourself and other people, "I doubt we can do it," say, "We will do it." Use your words to promote harmony, kindness, peace, and a friendly environment.
- **Offer support and encouragement:** Your words should help others choose the right path, reminding them of their goodness.
- **In anger, hold your tongue:** Silence heals. Even if someone is shouting at you, keep silent and listen. Reflect on your response, asking yourself, "Is what I want to say truthful and beneficial? Am I the right person to say it? Is this the right time?" As the father of our nation rightly said, "Speak only if it improves upon the silence."

Hack 34: Timeless Wisdom:

The *Bhagavad Gita* teaches self-inquiry and transformative action rather than responding heatedly at the moment:

- **Self-awareness:** Notice not only what you say but also how you say it. Ask yourself, "How do I feel after certain remarks? How do the recipients of those remarks react?"
- **Self-inquiry:** If you often feel compelled to say hurtful or derogatory things, ask, "What makes me say what I say? What emotions am I suppressing? Is what I'm saying true? How can I deal with this situation without harsh words?"

"You become attractive once you stop caring about being attractive, and focus on becoming a better person instead."

13

BEING ATTRACTIVE

> *"Character is a quality that embodies many important traits, such as integrity, courage, perseverance, confidence, and wisdom. Unlike your fingerprints that you are born with and can't change. Character is something that you create within yourself and must take responsibility for changing." – Jim Rohn*

We all want others to be drawn to us so we can make friends, date, and be given opportunities. According to *New York Times* bestselling author John Medina, the human brain has a short but efficient attention span. We are attracted to people and things that are intriguing, exciting, and engaging.

The key is to make a memorable first impression within 30 seconds. Here, we examine what makes a person attractive and offer practical approaches to increase your magnetism.

Let's begin by debunking two widespread misconceptions: first, that physical beauty is the most important thing, and second, that looking good is the same as being beautiful.

While dressing and grooming well are imperative, you must also have a friendly disposition, integrity, and kindness to be likable. In other words, you must have an attractive character.

The Attraction Checklist:

To cultivate a good personality, you must master certain soft skills and work on your appearance and behavior. Here is a list of must-haves:

- **Be authentic:** Stay true to yourself and your values. Don't pretend to like the latest trends because "that's cool." Don't put on facades to get people to like you or pretend that you're perfect.

Everyone has flaws. The right thing to do is fix them, not hide them. For example, if you are prone to snapping at people, work on controlling your anger.

- **Refine your social skills:** Effective communication, empathy, and respect are mandatory for everyone. Learn conflict resolution and relationship management. For example, in a conversation, listen and don't interrupt.

  Hold space for the other person; make them feel seen and heard. Avoid sarcasm if the other person is not fond of it. Ensure that you're not offending anyone and that you are well-informed.

- **Improve your body language:** A friendly, formal smile can never go wrong when you make eye contact. It's ideal when you want to start a conversation. Make sure that you appear confident and secure. Walk tall, avoid slouching, and reduce the number of hand gestures.

- **Maintain a calm disposition:** No one likes people who gripe or yell, who are argumentative, stressed-out, and scattered. Learn to control your temper and reactivity.

  When you feel anxious or need to exhibit compulsive behavior, remove yourself from the social situation. Go to a place where you can be alone and calm down.

- **Believe in yourself:** If you don't believe in yourself, how can you expect others to put faith in you? Know your strengths and communicate them effectively, especially in interviews or when building new relationships. Take constructive criticism from credible people who mean well, such as experts or mentors.

- **Humility is always welcome:** Make sure that you do not appear overly proud, self-important, or boastful. Be confident but modest – this will attract people to you.

  Be welcoming and willing to teach others without making it a big deal; you will earn their respect and admiration. You can indulge in a bit of self-deprecating humor as long as it doesn't turn into a pity party all the time.

- **Be assertive:** Operate on the principle of mutual respect; don't be a pushover or doormat. Call out bad behavior, foul language, ill-treatment, etc. Treat yourself and others with dignity – this is imperative for survival.

- **Be positive:** Look for silver linings and encourage people to do the same. Be someone who does not cower in the face of a challenge. At the same time, don't promote toxic positivity; one can't always be positive in the face of adversity. If a colleague is unreasonable, don't assume they will start behaving reasonably at some point. By speaking to them about their behavior, you are taking positive action.

- **Don't be boring, annoying, or whiny:** The goal of any conversation should be that both parties derive enjoyment and information from each other. It could be as simple as making the other person laugh.

  Don't be drab and repetitive. Ensure that what you say is original. Don't parrot statistics and small talk starters. Be creative and compliment people upon starting a conversation. Whining will tire the other person, and they will avoid spending time with you.

- **Show respect and empathy:** Avoid talking over and interrupting people – this is rude behavior. Do not patronize anyone. Treat everyone with dignity and respect at all times.

  If someone opens up to you about something, do not invalidate their experience; listen with understanding and compassion.

- **Take care of your external appearance**: This is an intrinsic part of your personality and being attractive. How you present yourself to the world matters. Groom and dress well all the time. Keep it classy and elegant.

  Don't show up to a work meeting in a flashy dress or low-rise jeans. The rule of thumb is wearing what is appropriate for the occasion. The key is to look confident and feel comfortable.

If you make the above suggestions a daily practice, they will become second nature eventually. Suffice to say that being attractive is vital to thriving because it ensures that you make the right connections and build quality relationships.

Here are a few hacks to help you:

Hack 35: The Attraction Cheat-Sheet:

The following body language signs will help you ascertain whether people are attracted to you. When someone finds you appealing and engaging:

- They lean in.
- They tilt their head while talking to you.
- They smile at you.
- They make eye contact with you.
- They observe and attentively listen to you.

Of course, you can signal to other people that you find them engaging by using the same body language, making you more attractive. Everyone enjoys being appreciated.

Hack 36: Brush Up on Your Manners and Etiquette:

Even if your manners and etiquette are up to par, ensure that you are keeping up with the times. Adhere to other cultures' social norms and customs, especially if you are doing business with people from other countries. Learn things such as politically correct terminology, greetings, pronoun use, gifting, tipping, formalities, etc.

Hack 37: Personality Development Classes:

These courses teach you to identify your weaknesses and strengths. They help you become the best version of yourself. Whether you are starting from scratch or want to polish yourself, they can be useful.

TAKE CHARGE OF YOUR FINANCES

Begin your journey towards a secured future

"Every little bit counts, so rather than looking for one big way to save a ton of money, save in lots of small ways and set yourself up for success."

14

MONEY FUNDAMENTALS

"Money isn't the most important thing in life, but it's reasonably close to oxygen on the 'gotta have it' scale."
-Zig Ziglar

In the previous sections of this book, we explored the fundamental conditions for thriving – living with intent and purpose, and being our best selves. Many see prosperity as synonymous with living our best lives, but it is not. Money is a tool, which helps us survive and thrive in the world.

Despite that it is a necessity, we are all under-equipped regarding money matters to some degree. We were never taught financial literacy, which is both our right and responsibility. The three key components of money management are having a mindset of abundance, understanding how money works, and attaining financial freedom. Let's look at them more closely.

Developing the Abundance Mindset:

Everyone desires prosperity, but not everyone's definition is the same. For some, it means millions; for others, it's having enough to have peace of mind. Neither is achievable without a mindset of abundance. Personal finance expert Suze Orman in her book, *9 Steps to Financial Freedom*, shows how money issues are linked to subconscious fears about success formed in childhood; in other words, the problem is psychological at its root.

Her solution is the time-tested prosperity law of paying yourself first – a practice that, in addition to building wealth, also fosters self-worth. Usually, when people get their paychecks, they pay their bills, putting little or nothing aside for themselves. While this will help you become debt-free sooner, it may not offer you financial freedom.

To build personal wealth, you need to put away money in a savings account or invest it for higher returns.

The key is to keep it where it's more difficult to spend it. Furthermore, paying yourself is empowering because it drills into your mind that:

> ➤ You're more important than a credit card company.
> ➤ You're making financial freedom your priority.
> ➤ You're applying sound financial practices.

The more your savings grow, the more empowered you will be to make the right career choices (instead of desperate ones). By overcoming any psychological blocks related to abundance, you put yourself on the road to prosperity.

Understanding How Money Works:

To have a sound financial future and attain financial freedom, you must demystify money management. Anthony Robbins defines money management as a strategy that enables you to get the most returns on your income. It comprises budgeting, investing, and saving in such a way that you get the highest growth. Here's what you need to know:

- **Budget:** Begin by tracking all your expenses, categorizing your purchases, and evaluating them in terms of priority. Then divide your budget into three parts: debts, essentials, and paying yourself.
  Set a limit to your spending and cut back as much as you can on non-essentials, like entertainment and luxury products. Do your best to reduce the cost of utilities, like finding a cheaper internet package. Debts and interests eat away all your income. To pay them off faster, consider the snowball technique, where you start by paying off the smallest debt and then move on to the next larger one. This method gives you a sense of accomplishment while helping you become debt-free.

- **Invest:** It's a common misconception that only the rich invest. You can start with as little as $500. Even if you make $1 per week on it, in 20 years, you would have over $1000. Learn as much as you can about investing before you get into the game. You can consult a professional, and there are many apps to help you. Author Raja Sekharan points out that most people assume that they can be rich by saving and cutting expenses. The ideal approach is making your money work for you by applying this formula:
    - In your 20s and 30s, work hard and grow your income – also focus on learning to invest.
    - In your 30s and 40s, your investments will be working for you.
    - In your 40s, you can achieve financial freedom from your job due to passive income from investments.
- **Save:** Save every week or month; create a "rainy day" fund. Make saving part of your monthly budget, aiming to have a sizable amount within a specific timeframe. Saving for something greater than yourself, like providing for your family, will help you stay motivated.

Attaining Financial Freedom:

We often misunderstand the term "financial freedom" as the ability to buy anything we want or never having to work. Neither is correct. Financial freedom means having enough money to cover all your expenses so that you don't have to work mundane jobs; instead, you can work on your passion projects. Achieving this can be a long process, but rest assured that it is possible with planning and consistent effort.

To attain financial freedom, you need to be debt-free, have a contingency fund, and have adequate medical insurance. Your income, usually passive, must come from investments made early in life. Ultimately, you must have good money habits. According to author Robert Kiyosaki, these are budgeting, spending mindfully, taking responsibility, having clear financial goals, and learning continuously. Here's an inspiring story to illustrate:

> *Camilo Maldonado was raised in poverty, never taught how to manage money at home or school. When he went to college and handled his own finances, he began using a money management app to track his spending. Knowing how much he spent in all areas — meals, entertainment, travel — changed everything. "When I graduated and got my first job, I was already comfortable with living within my means. That experience in college fundamentally changed my attitude toward money," says Maldonado, now a co-founder of The Finance Twins.*

> *"If you don't track where your money is going, you'll never be able to master your financial situation. You don't have to use a fancy program. You can start with your bank and credit card statements and a blank sheet of paper. It's that simple,"* he says.

Now that you have the gist of money management, you can improve your finances and thrive.

The following hacks will help you put your money matters in order:

Hack 38: Play by the Rule:

The 70/30 rule, as defined by Jim Rohn, is a good habit to adopt. After paying taxes, 70% of your income needs to go to expenditures. The remaining 30% needs to be divided into three parts and allocated to capital investment, charity, and savings. Adopt this method every month to save more, earn from your wealth, and give back to the community.

Hack 39: Access All Available Resources:

You do not have to study economics or be an investment manager to manage and invest your money.

- In the internet age, educating yourself on how money works has never been easier. You can access endless resources, either inexpensively or free of charge – books, courses, lectures, etc. Keep in mind, however, that the learning never stops.
- If you cannot hire a personal finance manager yet, you can access free information and advice from sources like local banks. Make an appointment with a bank-level financial advisor and ask questions. See what investments they have to offer. With that said, banks will only offer their products, which may not be the most competitive or lucrative on the market. Even if you buy a term deposit for six months, your money will be earning something while you shop around for a better rate.
- Use technology to manage your wealth in a hassle-free and effective manner. Apps can help you budget and invest on a single device. Your financial information is no longer stored in reams of paper.

15

SPEND v/s SAVE v/s INVEST

"Don't tell me where your priorities are. Show me where you spend your money, and I'll tell you what they are." - James W. Frick

Unless you are a billionaire with the ability to burn money without making a dent in your wealth, living comfortably throughout your life is predicated on spending, saving, and investing wisely. Such decisions tend to be difficult for most people due to the lack of financial literacy. This chapter will give an overview of the what, why, and how of spending, saving, and investing.

Spend Mindfully:

"To spend, or not to spend?" is the question that plagues us all. Even if you earn exorbitant sums of money, you will be in trouble before long if you spend foolishly. Spend carefully after deliberating the pros and cons. The rule of thumb is, "If you gain from buying something, go ahead."

For example, you can spend on:

- **Essentials**: It goes without saying that you can spend on food, clothing, and shelter. Just ensure that it is not all luxury items and frequently.
  It is okay to spend on premium quality for high-ticket items that need to last you a long time, like an oven or dishwasher. However, pay for quality, not a brand name.
- **Health:** Get a gym membership or a diet plan from a nutritionist to stay healthy and fit. Buy health insurance for yourself and your family.
  It is alright to spend on quality products that contribute to your health, like high-quality mattresses and healthy food.
- **Joy and well-being:** Studies show that people who spend money on experiences are happier than those who splurge on things. In regards to travel, opt for sightseeing instead of staying in a 5-star-hotel.
  If you have tension headaches from sitting in front of the computer all day, pay for a professional massage.
- **Education:** Don't shy away from spending on the education of your children and yourself.
  Again, look for free/cheaper alternatives. But if an expensive certificate course is necessary to upskill, then do it. See it as an investment – the better skills you have, the more you can earn.
- **Professional advice, especially on finances:** Spend money to increase your income or pay for a professional who will help you invest better. If you are filing your own tax returns, consider hiring a tax accountant to help you find additional savings.

Avoid Unnecessary Spending:

Any good financial advisor will tell you that you must not splurge. This does not mean that you have to become miserly or deprive yourself. The following tips will help curtail unnecessary spending:

- Don't step into a shop without a list. Stick to buying only the listed items. Avoid impulse shopping on sites like Amazon, Flipkart, Asos, etc. Be careful of promotional offers and advertisements. Avoid credit cards.
- If you use one, don't buy anything you can't repay fully within one month's cycle.
- Avoid late credit card payments like the plague.

Save For a Rainy Day and Earn:

The golden rule is to start by setting aside six months of expenses for emergencies, like job loss, reduced pay, or medical expenses. Next, set aside another 6-12 months of expenses. This emergency fund should earn a decent amount of interest; however, one portion should be easy to cash out if you need it. You can create this flexibility through term deposits. You can also max out all your retirement schemes, company gratuities, EPF, etc.

Invest Intelligently:

Rather than you working for money, you should have your money work for you. Here are a few investment vehicles to consider:

- **Stocks:** Also known as shares or equity, they entitle the holder to a proportion of the issuing corporation's earnings. You can purchase stocks through online stockbrokers. Buy only high-quality shares and make sure that you are financially literate before you begin investing. Be clear about the kind of risks you are willing to take. Finances are not everyone's cup of tea. If you want to play the field but are not keen on learning it, hire a professional to guide you. Or hire an expert financial advisor whose job will be to help you make money. Pick someone with credentials and opt for a variable commission plan – the more money they make for you, the higher their compensation. If you decide to invest in stocks, remember not to be emotional about it. Stay in for the long haul. Take note from Warren Buffet, "If you aren't willing to own a stock for ten years, don't even think about owning it for ten minutes."
- **Mutual funds:** According to Investopedia, mutual funds pool money from the investing public to buy securities, usually stocks and bonds. A mutual fund share represents an investment in different stocks or other securities instead of a single holding. Unlike stocks, mutual fund shares do not give their holders voting rights. Mutual funds are relatively less volatile than stocks. They also earn less than shares. To my mind, this is ideal for the majority of novice investors. In fact, finance websites recommend the same because mutual funds enable investors to put their money into many stocks with a single transaction. They advise dedicating as little as 5% of your portfolio to stocks for the thrill of it after you have made a significant amount from mutual funds. What is more, nowadays, there are many AI-based platforms, which intelligently manage mutual funds. This has resulted in a significant increase in returns compared to traditional mutual funds.

- **Real estate and REITs:** The next two prominent vehicles are real estate and real estate mutual funds (REITs). The former is stable but illiquid; it takes time to sell a property, so it's not ideal if you find yourself in a bind. Also, the rental yield is not very predictable and can stagnate. You need to do a great deal of research before investing here. Real Estate Investment Trusts (REITs) are better because they work like mutual funds. You own a portion of the real estate asset class without being tied up in it for a long time. Ultimately, it is critical to understand that if you invest, it will be a long-term play. You can create significant wealth if you stay in the investment game for 10-20 years, but this isn't for you if you are averse to time and risk. With that said, without investments, wealth creation is difficult.

If you decide to take the plunge, read the following books to inform yourself:

- *Money* by Tony Robbins
- *Get Rich and Retire Early* by Raja Sekharan (for Indian stocks)
- *The Intelligent Investor* by Benjamin Graham
- *Rich Dad, Poor Dad* by Robert Kiyosaki
- *One Up on Wall Street* by Peter Lynch

Here are a few sure-fire hacks to put you on the road to financial freedom:

Hack 40: Avoid Debt Like the Plague:

Buying on credit isn't very smart. Shop with cash and debit cards only. If you cannot repay the full amount of your credit card balance, then cancel it or pay it off and set it aside for a rainy day.

Hack 41: Invest First; Spend Later:

Make your investments and savings monthly and automatic. Invest in equities but be prepared to remain in the game for years.

Hack 42: Avoid Withdrawing Retirement Funds:

Make it difficult to withdraw from your retirement fund by placing it in long-term fixed deposits. Choose annuities that are illiquid and offer substantial income.

16

BEING ASSET-LIGHT

"It's not how much money you make, but how much money you keep, how hard it works for you, and how many generations you keep it for."
- Robert Kiyosaki

The term "asset-light" refers to companies with relatively few capital assets compared to their value, like Airbnb, Uber, OYO, and Ola. The advantage of this business model is that they make as much money as possible while holding minimal assets, which can turn into liabilities.

For example, real estate value may drop if the market takes a nosedive; moreover, buildings need constant upkeep. Applying this business model to your life ensures that you curtail unnecessary spending and save more.

Spend Less by Being Asset-Light:

The average salaried employee in India spends at least 60% of their earnings on basic needs like shelter, transport, and repaying debt. The way out of this money pit is reducing expenditures and liabilities on the big-ticket items.

- **Homes:** People spend a considerable chunk of their earnings on their house, especially if they see it as a status symbol. Maintaining gardens and pools is expensive to the point that the asset may become a liability.
  When buying a house, focus on your needs. If you're a couple, 1 BHK suffices or probably a 2BHK, if you have regular visitors. Do not compromise on security, accessibility to amenities like stores and hospitals, and commute to work.

This may cost more, but you'll save time and money on travel and increase your quality of life. Avoid the fad of buying a vacation home unless it's an investment with substantial returns. You can rent it out or make it available to services like OYO and Airbnb. Also, if you have a spare room in your home, rent it and stuff the income into your savings.

- **Cars:** While real estate is likely to appreciate with time, a new car starts depreciating the moment you drive it off the lot. When buying this other big status symbol, again focus on your needs. If you don't drive every day, then don't buy a car; use an Uber. If you drive daily or weekly, consider a well-maintained second-hand vehicle. It will be at least 30% lesser than a brand new car.
- **Furniture, appliances:** Avoid spending excessively on unnecessary luxuries like grand décor. Websites like OLX connect sellers and buyers, especially for household items like furniture, exercise, equipment, etc.
- **Fashion, luxury goods, electronics, etc.:** You can buy pre-loved fashion and jewelry or clear the clutter in your home by giving things away or selling them. Check online stores when you're looking for things like electronics and books.
- **Businesses:** Brick-and-mortar businesses and those that require holding inventory are a liability. Robert Kiyosaki, the author of *Rich Dad, Poor Dad*, advises creating profit liquidity income instead. This means investing in something like oil to make a recurring profit instead of setting up a business. You can sell a dropping stock at the touch of a button but selling a home or business takes months. If you want a business, consider e-commerce models like drop-shipping, where you hold no inventory.

Use the Sharing Economy to Save and Earn:

You can save and earn even more through the sharing economy. A sharing economy is when two or more parties use technology to exchange goods and services. This constantly evolving model is expected to grow. In his blog, Peter Diamandis predicts that, by 2025, eight billion people will be hyper-connected through the internet. This means that more money will flow into tech, and more will be earned through it by:

- Freelancing, which enables even salaried employees to have a side-hustle. Trading goods and services, like in the traditional barter system. For example, if you are a cameraperson, you can trade services with an editor to help you both complete your film projects.

- Utilizing underused assets and skills, for instance, if you work as an accountant, you can create a website to sell your artwork. Crowdfunding and crowdsourcing can help you raise money for passion projects.
- Co-working and co-branding; if you want to increase the reach of your YouTube channel, you can collaborate with a like-minded channel to create content. Picture this: If Warren Buffet and Robert Kiyosaki talked about money and investments, wouldn't we tune in? We would even pay if the content were of premium quality.
- Participating in the shared economy will increase your reach and riches and enable collaboration – this is a win-win for all.

The following hacks will help you embrace asset-light living:

Hack 43: Spend Less; Keep More:

- Buy fewer things and only what you absolutely need. Buy second-hand items whenever you can. Purchase major assets based on needs, not as status symbols. Sell them if there is a risk of them becoming a liability.
- Sell big assets you do not regularly use (e.g., car, boat, vacation home) and invest the money where you can yield high returns. Choose profit income liquidity over setting up a business.

Hack 44: Share More; Earn More:

- Earn extra income from under-utilized skills. Rent out spare rooms or second homes. If you own a car, earn by freelancing on Uber as a driver on weekends or days convenient to you.

Hack 45: Mind the Pitfalls:

It's crucial to use technology to save money as long as you are mindful of the following:

- Online stores make shopping super easy and tempting. Before making a purchase, make sure that this is something you truly need or want. Beware of clickbait and relentless advertising. Try not to fall for it.
- Run specific searches only for things you need. Once you have all the information, unsubscribe from promotional emails, or you will be inundated with emails, ads, suggestions, etc.

"Money is multiplied in practical value depending on the number of W's you control in your life: what you do, when you do it, where you do it, and with whom you do it."
- Timothy Ferriss

17

INCREASING YOUR EARNING POTENTIAL

"If you don't find a way to make money while you sleep, you will work until you die." - Warren Buffett

In a blog post, Randy Gage points out that it's not a sin to be born poor but to stay destitute. It is everyone's right and responsibility to become financially independent. Saving, investing, and living asset-light goes a long way, but you also have to earn more because, typically, the largest portion of a person's income goes to living expenses and debts.

To understand the importance of earning more, let's start by redefining the word "job." In *Rich Dad, Poor Dad*, Robert Kiyosaki defines it as "j-ust o-ver b-roke" because most salaried employees live within their means all their lives, working and paying bills. One day, they retire and realize that their primary income has vanished. According to a 2017 report on CareerBuilder, 78% of Americans live from paycheck to paycheck. This means that they can be homeless within two months if they lose their job.

> Living Paycheck to Paycheck is a Way of Life for Majority of U.S. Workers, According to New CareerBuilder Survey
>
> Study Highlights:
> - 78 percent of U.S. workers live paycheck to paycheck to make ends meet
> - Nearly one in 10 workers making $100,000+ live paycheck to paycheck
> - More than 1 in 4 workers do not set aside any savings each month
> - Nearly 3 in 4 workers say they are in debt today - more than half think they will always be
> - More than half of minimum wage workers say they have to work more than one job to make ends meet

Source: http://press.careerbuilder.com/2017-08-24-Living-Paycheck-to-Paycheck-is-a-Way-of-Life-for-Majority-of-U-S-Workers-According-to-New-CareerBuilder-Survey

Financial independence means that you have enough passive income, typically through investments, to pay all your expenses without working a 9-5 job. Does that sound like "pie in the sky"? Well, I am here to tell you that you can achieve it within five years by creating passive income, following frugal principles of FIRE, and applying the Law of Compensation.

Passive Income Demystified:

Most people do not have multiple sources of income. In fact, 95% don't even think it's necessary. They appear content with what they make from their jobs, not understanding that additional income can be passive and replace their salary. Any passive income idea requires a sizable investment and nurturing initially. It will grow with hard work and time, bringing consistent revenue with little effort. Aim to have at least 20 sources of income, each with the potential to earn 10% of your current income in five years, at which point you should have enough recurring income to quit your job if you wish to do so.

Here are a few ways to create passive income:

- **Dividend stocks:** Dividend-yielding stocks are among the most common sources of passive income. For every stock you own, you are paid a portion of the company's profits. For example, if a company offers a 12% dividend, then as a shareholder, for every 100 shares, you receive an additional 15.
- **Certificate deposits:** If you are risk-averse, then CDs will work best for you. They are offered by banks and require low investment. They are ideal if you have just started working and can save a little. The longer the deposit, the higher the rate of interest.
- **Create and sell online content.** The online world has an insatiable appetite for content, which can be monetized. By no means an exhaustive list, the following are a few ideas to get your creative juices flowing:
  - **Ebooks.** Everyone is a writer these days, and self-publishing is common. Platforms like Amazon help you publish and sell your books. A good book is timeless and will get you a significant amount of returns.
  - **Online courses.** You may have taken one yourself on platforms like Udemy or Shaw's Academy. If you are an expert in some area, you can build and teach a course. These are reasonably priced and widely promoted. As long as the course remains relevant, you are bound to get students.

- o **Stock photos:** If you are a talented photographer, then it's time to make money off your gift. List yourself on sites like Shuttershock, Getty, or Stock and sell your images to newspapers, magazines, and other companies. Good photos will fetch a significant amount consistently.

- **Get involved in e-commerce:** You can take advantage of the digital economy by selling products online. Make sure you select a product category you like and know something about; for example, if you are interested in health and wellness, sell related products either by setting up an e-commerce site or selling through platforms like Amazon or eBay.
- **Sell digital art and crafts online:** Designers of all sorts (e.g., graphics, illustration, furniture, accessories, clothing) sell their creations on platforms like Etsy. This essentially means that you are turning your hobby into a business while getting exposure to your work.
- **Explore cashbacks:** When you make purchases, go for deals that offer cashback through e-wallet payments. You can also look at apps that pay you if you install them on your devices. You will save on purchases and earn rewards.

The FIRE Model:

As the name indicates, the goal of the Financial Independence, Retire Early (FIRE) movement is financial independence and early retirement. The model, which gained traction through online communities, is based on aggressively maximizing savings. It suggests the 4% rule as a withdrawal guideline, setting a goal of at least 25 times one's estimated annual expenses. Assuming constant income and expenses, and not counting investment returns, the model shows that:

- o Saving 10%, it takes nine years of work to save for one year of living expenses. Saving 25%, it takes three years of work to save for one year of living expenses. Saving 50%, it takes one year of work to save for one year of living expenses. Saving 75%, it takes four months of work to save for one year of living expenses.

Conversely, if you spend 100% or more of your income, then you won't save anything and will keep working all your life. If you spend 0% of your income and live for free, you do need not worry. If – like most people – you don't have the resources to do that, save at least 10% of your income. Invest it in places that yield high returns so it can snowball.

If this passive income enables you to manage your expenses and inflation for the rest of your life, as well as save for further investments, then you can retire. The general rule is to have a net worth that is 25% times your living expenses. If you attain this magic number, you are considered financially independent.

The Law of Compensation:

You need an adequate salary with regular increments to become financially independent within a reasonable amount of time – this means increasing your earning potential by applying the Law of Compensation, as explained by Bob Proctor.

The law states that the amount of money an individual makes is directly proportional to:

- The need for what they do in a marketplace.
- Their ability to do it.
- The difficulty of replacing them.

Analyze your situation by asking questions like, "Is what I do relevant today? Are my skills in demand? Can I switch companies with the same skillset and get better pay?" If all the answers are yes, that's good. Then ask, "Am I the best in the industry? How qualified and experienced am I? Do I bring significant value to my employer?"

Again, if the answers are yes, then you're doing great. If the answers were no, you might want to learn market-relevant skills or use your current skills differently. For instance, if you're getting paid less as a print journalist, explore digital journalism.

Here are a few hacks to help you improve your earning potential and thrive:

Hack 46: Don't Sell Yourself Short:

If you think you deserve a raise at work, ask for it. The worst that can happen is that you won't get it. Start raising your hourly rates when you have enough ongoing clients if you are running a freelance business.

Hack 47: Upskill and Offer Exceptional Service:

It's critical to leverage your current employment situation fully. Always focus on creating value for the company you work for, and the money will follow.

Hack 48: Make Your Money Earn:

Start with simple things like switching to a savings account that pays you the highest interest on deposits. Invest as much as you can. Avoid withdrawing from your investments and make it a rule to only add to them.

Hack 49: Create Active Income Streams:

Take side-gigs but be ethical about moonlighting. Also, look for income outside of the skillset that you use in your job. For example, monetize your blog, sell your art, or get involved in e-commerce.

Hack 50: Create Passive Income Streams:

Try to create one new source of passive income every month, like dividend stocks and rentals.

"Beware of small expenses; a small leak will sink a great ship."
- Benjamin Franklin.

TAKE CHARGE OF YOUR CAREER

Follow your passion —your life, your choice!

"You are responsible for your life. You can't keep blaming somebody else for your dysfunction. Life is really about moving on."
— Oprah Winfrey

18

THE CAREER CONUNDRUM

"The only way to do great work is to love what you do. If you haven't found it yet, keep looking. Don't settle." – Steve Jobs

This section of the book examines what it takes to thrive in the workplace, beginning with that soul-crushing feeling of being stuck professionally. The following chapters, *"Be valuable"*, *"Be service-minded"*, and *"Be a consummate professional"* examine how to get unstuck and enjoy a rewarding career by making yourself an asset. *"Be visible"* shows you how to increase your cachet.

Even if you are an invaluable employee, this will not translate into money and success if your contribution is not recognized. The last two chapters endeavor to inspire you to move past the "little-me" employee mentality and your immediate needs into a grander vision for your career and future. But let's begin with what I call the "career conundrum," which is nothing less than a pandemic in itself!

Even before COVID-19, at least 75% of the American workforce across all industries was unhappy with their jobs, not feeling recognized, experiencing loneliness and stress. Coupled with the sinking economies, all this creates a conundrum that affects almost the entire workforce.

If you are in such a predicament, it may be time to review and reconsider alternate career paths, selecting one that offers satisfaction, appropriate compensation, and learning opportunities – this is crucial to thriving.

Growth is painful.
Change is painful.
But, nothing is as painful as staying stuck where you do not belong.
- *N. R. Narayana Murthy*

How to Know If It's Time to Change Careers:

You want a more meaningful or better-paying job. You may feel that your talents are being wasted or dread going to work. Even if you relate to all these scenarios, "jumping ship" cannot be an impulsive decision.

The following suggestions will help you assess both timing and options:

- **Problems and solutions:** Start by identifying what is preventing you from making a change, as well as the consequences and remedies. If money is the key issue, set up an emergency fund to help you meet your expenses. Do not jump without a safety net.
- **Market research and soul-search:** Research the job market before you resign, focusing on the areas in which you are skilled, as well as those that interest you even if you do not possess the necessary skills yet. The goal is not merely to get another job but to find a life path that will help you thrive.
- **Explore and learn:** If you want a career change but don't know what that is, then meet people, take courses, and explore options before quitting. This will give you a better understanding of what prospective jobs entail to avoid ending up in something you dislike.
- **Hit the ground running:** After you resign, start looking for work immediately. Focus on connecting with people in addition to traditional job hunting.

In short, you should not quit a steady income without a clear understanding of the job market and economic conditions, as well as your finances and prospects.

How to Choose the Correct Career Path:

To thrive in life, you need to be happy at your job, which is where you will spend most of your day. In setting that as your destination, consider the basics of career-building outlined below:

- **Know thyself:** Some people are relatively comfortable working jobs that are meaningless to them. They become good at tolerating bad situations in the name of stability. Some do not seek their "bliss" because they do not explore their talents that may lead to opportunities. Only you know what makes you happy. Consider alternatives based on your qualifications, skills, and interests. Compare past work experiences.

Which was best suited to your skills and interests? Which position made you happy, allowed you to get out of your comfort zone and grow? Which jobs are in demand? How do you feel about factors like safety, working hours, etc.? Narrow down your choices but prioritize safety, skills, and job satisfaction over money unless you have heavy financial responsibilities.

- **The three fundamentals:** There are three things to look for in choosing a career path. The first is a sense of accomplishment or mastery of a skill. People need to cultivate, improve, and be recognized for their abilities.

  The second is good company culture. People want to build professional relationships and benefit from them in a healthy, supportive, and respectful environment. The third and most crucial element is a sense of purpose.

  We all need to do something meaningful because that is profoundly connected to our identity.

  In an ideal world, one would have all three, but you may not be able to find them in one company. What can you compromise on? Because this is a tough choice, most people choose the "better devil," i.e., remaining in a toxic environment because they need the money, for example.

  However, research shows that money only marginally influences job satisfaction. This means that one is content when one learns or grows, or finds something meaningful.

- **Consider your values and lifestyle:** While compensation is important, it's not advisable to choose a career based on how much you might make. Instead, focus on what you want from life.

  Do you want to work alone or collaborate with people? Do you enjoy numbers or creative endeavors? Do you want to help others? How many hours are you willing to put in?

  Once you have the answers to these questions, find roles accordingly. Also, make sure that the career aligns with your values. For instance, if you're a criminal defense attorney, will you be able to defend all your clients, even if they are guilty?

- **Plan your career path:** Set short-term (a few months) and long-term (between two to five years) goals to delineate the path and the destination. These need to be specific, measurable, attainable, relevant, and time-bound.

  For instance, if you're a journalist with two years' experience, your short-term goal might be learning storytelling through videos. Your long-term goal might be launching your own digital media channel. Be realistic about timelines but work hard. It's okay if your priorities change over time.

- **Equip yourself for your new career:** Upskill, train, and stay relevant so you can live up to your potential. A good example of this is the entrepreneurship bandwagon. Every year, many decide to become their own boss. Very few succeed.
  Even if they do not fail outright, they end up earning less and working more. There are many reasons for this; you may be an incredible home cook, but that does not mean you know how to run a restaurant. You need to get the necessary training. By all means, have a grand goal but also be realistic and self-aware.

Considering the above factors will not only help you overcome the career conundrum but also thrive. Here are a few hacks to help with the process:

Hack 51: Explore Job Crafting:

Job crafting refers to employees redesigning and reimagining their jobs to increase satisfaction. This is especially useful when you cannot quit a mundane position.
Job crafting is usually done by:

- **Changing functions:** For instance, an accountant may devise a better method for filing taxes to reduce repetition and improve efficiency.
- **Shifting peer relationships:** A computer engineer may teach advanced computer skills to a colleague, creating interaction and learning opportunities for both parties. If the engineer enjoys teaching, he can develop tutorials either for his workplace or online.
- **Shifting perspective:** No job is too menial; every role provides value – this cannot be stressed enough! Even if you are not working your dream job, you are contributing to society, or you would not be paid. For example, a hospital janitor may see his role as vital instead of dull because it contributes to the patient's safety.

Hack 52: Put Good Advice to Practice:

To do well at work, consider the following advice from leaders in the corporate world. Make sure to track the changes you experience while implementing these recommendations.

- **Don't be paralyzed by fear:** Take risks, plan, and push yourself to achieve what you can. Know that you're capable of anything. Fear only holds you back, so tame it.

- **To err is human:** Know that you are not your mistakes. Pick yourself up and keep going.
- **Manage your career and decide for yourself:** Don't do what others are doing. Listen to criticism with a pinch of salt. Your job needs to be defined based on what you want and not what others have.
- **Learn something new every day:** Read an article to improve your knowledge or sign up for a course that will either help you upskill or make a career shift.
- **Never attach your self-worth to your job:** Sure, doing well at work improves self-esteem, but knowing that you are not your job is critical. You are of value, irrespective of having a career.

"You attitude is like a price tag. It shows how valuable you are."

19

BEING VALUABLE

"We get paid for bringing value to the marketplace. It takes time... but we get paid for the value, not the time." - Jim Rohn

Career gurus say that the key to moving up the career ladder is to be sought-after and indispensable. The phrase "value-driven" is tossed around a great deal, but not many understand what it means.

Understanding Value:

Being value-driven means that you contribute to the organization by being exceptionally good at what you do. The specifics vary greatly from one position to another, for example, between a salesperson and cardiologist.

Even so, there are shared factors, which Peter Voogd delineates as follows:

- **Expertise:** Narrow down the skills you want to master and then consistently practice them while learning from your competitors. For example, if you're an HR professional, read up on current work culture, laws, and workforce issues. This will help you create innovative solutions to scout for talent and retain employees.
- **Productivity and efficiency:** No, they are not the same thing. Productivity is how much work you get done: quantity. Efficiency is how well you do it: quality. Ideally, you must get a significant amount of good quality work done in a day. If you're a reporter, you may need to file about five powerful stories every week to be considered a sought-after journalist with gravitas.

- **Organization:** Being organized includes but is not limited to your ability to schedule and accomplish things. It feeds directly into productivity and efficiency. It can extend beyond your personal habits to making the best use of technology, for example. Installing an inventory management system is expensive, but it saves staff hours spent on taking inventory, reducing loss, and streamlining your operations.
- **Reputation:** You need to be known for the quality of your work and your integrity – this is not something you can fake; you must live up to your reputation. If you want to be known as a great website designer, you must have sites to show prospective clients. If you're starting out, find ways to build your portfolio by making sites for friends at a low rate, etc.
- **Influence:** You must have the ability to persuade others and inspire them to do better. Your ideas must be creative but achievable; they should contribute to the organization. For instance, if you are a copywriter at a creative agency, you might create an Instagram page that posts jokes. As you gain traction, you will be marketing yourself and your company.
- **Good personality:** To be a valuable employee, you must interact well with colleagues, clients, and supervisors. Being amiable is beneficial both for the business and for your advancement.
- **Positivity:** No one wants to work with negative people. Do not allow yourself to spiral into defeatism. Try to help others when they are down. Develop a growth mindset and believe that you can accomplish anything. Furthermore, pay attention to your weaknesses and find ways to turn them into strengths.

Train your mind to see the good in everything. Positivity is a choice. The happiness of your life depends on the quality of your thoughts.

- **Learn from the best:** At every opportunity, surround yourself with people who are better than you. Rather than feeling threatened, without feeling inferior, be with people who can teach you something new, preferably related to your industry.
- **Vision:** Irrespective of what position you have in the company, you must have the ability to look beyond the obvious. You must be able to foresee problems and have solutions ready, operating from the premise that the firm needs to grow and adapt continually.
Ensure that the quality of your work matches that vision. As a value-driven employee, you're working not just for the benefit of yourself but also for the company.

Do You Bring Value to the Table?

The points mentioned above, while simple, are not necessarily quantifiable because they are often open to interpretation. Business consultant Cy Wakeman, in her book *The Reality-Based Rules of the Workplace*, lists a set of questions that will help you determine whether you bring value to a firm or not:

- Am I consistent with the quality of my work and results?
- Am I improving every year? Am I moving ahead with purpose or resting on past laurels?
- Do I spend most of my work hours with the top performers?
- Have I added to the job description with my initiatives?
- Do I set goals beyond what has been established by my supervisors?
- Do I ask for regular feedback from my clients and supervisors?
- How does my performance compare to that of my peers?
- Do I collaborate at work and have excellent professional relationships?

Answer the above questions as honestly as you can, and rate yourself on a scale between one and five, one being the lowest and five the highest. If your total score is close to 45, then you are considered a high-value employee. If you score below 30, then work on becoming the best you can be.

How to Increase Your Value?

To climb the career ladder and ensure job security, consider implementing the following ideas and behaviors:

- Understand and support the goals of your employers. Your goals need to align with theirs for the company to do well. Both sides need to collaborate and teach each other.
- Foster trust and loyalty by looking out for your manager. Be on their side. Alert them about potential problems – this will help them solve the issues before they turn into blunders.
- Communicate proactively and efficiently. Keep your managers informed with regular, concise reports. Navigate the office gossip smartly. Steer clear of badmouthing your manager because it is unethical and detrimental to your advancement. If you find yourself in a sticky situation, go to your manager for help. Be prepared and ready to suggest a solution – this shows that you are accountable.

- Build bridges across the organization instead of burning them. Collaborate and communicate across departments and speak highly of your boss and manager. See yourself as a representative of your team.

How to Show That You Are Valuable?

Beyond being a valuable employee, you need to show that you're the one. While I dedicate an entire chapter to this topic, here are a few suggestions:

- Be confident in your abilities, praising yourself tactfully, and offering proof. For example, you can say that since you took over that sales territory, you have grown revenue 50% in one year. Ideally, your work must speak for itself, but a bit of modest bragging doesn't hurt.
- Be conscious that time is money. Spend more time on work and less on fluff. Be effective, efficient, organized, and result-driven.
- Inform your supervisor of the positive feedback you are receiving. Compile a package of "thank you" notes from clients and share it with your bosses and colleagues. Not only does this increase team morale, but it also tells people that you're an asset to the team.

Below are a few additional suggestions that you can put into practice:

Hack 53: Identify the Area of Your Desired Expertise:

You need to decide what you want to be known for and work towards it. It is usually easier to build on existing knowledge and skills, but that is not to say that you can't develop in a new area. For example, if you are already a good marketing copywriter, you may want to become an SEO expert.

Hack 54: Assess Your Skills and Gain Expertise:

Once you identify what area you want to gain expertise in, do an honest self-assessment.

- Are you the best? If not, how can you become the best?
- Research what the most successful professionals are doing.
- What can you learn from them?
- How can you improve your work based on their example?
- Most importantly, how can you develop your unique approach?
- How can you make yourself stand out?

Using the information you have gathered, create a plan to achieve your goal of being exceptional. Attend training sessions, upskilling programs, and practice as much as possible.

Hack 55: Keep Proving and Improving Your Expertise:

As already mentioned, keep your employers informed about your accomplishments. Showcase upskills by suggesting and implementing innovative approaches. Soon, your work will show results, and the recognition will begin. If the results aren't satisfactory, find where you're going wrong and fix it. Especially in today's rapidly shifting market, it's crucial not to fall asleep at the wheel. There is always room for improvement, even for experts.

Hack 56: Habits That Make You a Valuable Employee:

Even if you are not an expert in your field nor wish to be, the following suggestions will increase the value that you bring to your job every day:

- Be proactive. Work ahead of the curve. Foresee problems and solve them effectively.
- Finish things before the deadline – this allows enough time for revisions, improvements, additions, etc.
- Always make a plan and stick to it. If the situation changes, be flexible.
- Solve problems at their root, avoiding temporary fixes as much as possible.
- Commit only to what is achievable and do it exceptionally well.
- Always fight for what is right.

"Being of service to others is what brings true happiness."
- Marie Osmond

20

BEING SERVICE MINDED

"People do not care how much you know until they know how much you care."
—Teddy Roosevelt

While there are no shortcuts to success, having a service mindset is almost guaranteed to accelerate the journey. The basic premise of this approach is that you navigate your work interactions by asking the question, "How can I be of service?" When you operate from a service mindset, you strive to provide the best experience and results possible. As an employee, it means being value-driven, as outlined in the previous chapter. As an entrepreneur, it means going beyond selling a product or service to caring about your clients.

The Benefits of Having a Service Mindset:

Human beings are hardwired to be empathetic; this is how we have survived for eons in very challenging conditions. Beyond survival, there are many other benefits to being service-oriented, as we can see in the following examples:

- **More opportunities and money:** If you are a customer-care specialist who goes the extra mile, this gets you noticed by management, and soon you'll be up for a promotion. As an entrepreneur, providing an enhanced experience to your clients will increase your business through referrals and loyalty. If you're a student and job hunting, people who volunteer are looked upon favorably by recruiters. In all cases, your reward is growth, opportunity, and monetary gain.

- **Better performance and productivity:** If you have a service mindset as an employee, you become a valuable high-performer. As an employer, you give fair compensation to your employees and care about their well-being. For example, Zomato provided menstruation leaves for female employees. This well-received initiative sparked a conversation on taboo topics and encouraged industry leaders to focus more on their workers. Mental health holidays and counseling sessions at work are other ways employers try to be more inclusive and empathetic because they lead to increased productivity, loyalty, retention, etc.
- **Better relationships:** The service mindset enhances all social interactions and fosters more fulfilling professional relationships. Generous, helpful people are well-liked and have a reputation for being dependable and responsible.
- **Better health and well-being:** Research shows that students who volunteered in college had greater confidence and self-esteem than those who did not. Confidence and self-worth are something most adults struggle with; the more you care about others, the better you feel about yourself because you are making a positive impact in the world.

  In addition, when you help someone, your brain releases a feel-good hormone known as oxytocin, which creates feelings of love and trust. According to science, a healthy mind leads to a healthy body – this means being helpful and generous makes you healthier, gives life meaning, and alleviates depression.

How to Cultivate a Service Mindset:

The following suggestions will help you adopt this beneficial approach to your career and life:

- **Reciprocate:** The Law of Reciprocity, as delineated by Brian Tracy, states: "If you do something nice for me, I'll do something nice for you. I feel obligated to reciprocate." All human beings operate on this principle without even knowing it.
- You go to dinner with a colleague, and she insists on paying. Next time, you pick up the tab. **Two types of reciprocity come into play here:**
    - The first is financial and the second psychological, meaning that people feel good when someone treats them, and not good when one person pays all the time. The one who pays feels exploited, and the other feels embarrassed.

- **Engage emotionally, be authentic:** Even if you do not love your job, find aspects that you feel good about – it's important not only to appear but also to be engaged. If you are a team leader, make your colleagues feel valued by considering their ideas.

  If you are a freelancer, choose projects that resonate with you. For example, before agreeing to write copy for a brand, make sure that you believe in their product. If you are not engaged or genuine, it will become apparent soon enough. People sense inauthenticity and interpret it as an ulterior motive or obligation. Not only will this not win them over but likely to leave them with a bad experience.

- **Win people over:** "Treat your customers well. Value their time and money. Be attentive to their needs. Make them feel connected to your brand. Give meaning to their purchases." This advice is given to customer service specialists and salespeople. Kindness and expertise determine the customer's satisfaction and how they perceive the company or brand.

  This approach is key even if you are an employee or freelancer. Apply it to your personality by becoming a 'brand' yourself. Showcase your manners and expertise so that people come looking for you because you're the best.

The ideas mentioned above will help you develop a service-oriented mindset, which – in turn – will help you thrive. Here are a few hacks to make the process easy:

Hack 57: Adopt and Practice the Four Es:

- **Empathy**: Showing empathy means caring about other people's feelings and treating them with respect and kindness. Put yourself in their shoes, and listen to their concerns. This will not only make you a better person but you will also be perceived as an asset to the firm.
- **Education**: Take the time to educate yourself and your peers without being condescending. Also, educate your customers to help them make the best choice – being honest builds trust between buyers and sellers, leading to repeat business. Education also means being informed regarding inclusive language and behavior.
- **Ecosystem**: Being mindful of the ecosystem means creating a work environment that is positive, healthy, and conducive to helping others. Foster the service mindset in your workplace by practicing what you preach – this will encourage others to adopt a generous attitude.

- **Encouragement:** By helping people grow, you help yourself and your company. Recognize the efforts of others. Show your appreciation and motivate them with a nice gesture like buying lunch. Remember that success is a journey that everyone takes together.

Hack 58: Be of Service, Not Servile:

Being servile is a slippery slope that ends in being exploited, losing respect and self-respect, not being taken seriously, even being disliked by people who will view this behavior as disingenuous, cowardly, and desperate. So, how can you apply the Law of Reciprocity in the work environment without being servile? By looking for opportunities to help others. However, make sure you don't overdo it. For example, during negotiations, ask many questions without being annoying – this makes the other party feel that you care about their project. In the event of a disagreement, agree to the terms slowly and be fair. Make sure you communicate the importance of fairness.

Hack 59: Develop a Service-Oriented Persona:

To do this, you need to adopt and practice the following behaviors until they become personality traits:

- **Care and help:** Look out for clients and teammates. Help them as much as you can, within reason.
- **Make an effort:** Go out of your way to deliver the best results and create a positive work environment.
- **Make people feel valued:** Foster engagement by making your colleagues feel valued. Also, help them socialize.
- **Practice what you preach:** Teach by example. Take time to mentor juniors and help them grow. At the same time, keep working on yourself.

Hack 60: Ask and Listen:

Knowing how to ask questions and listening is critical in any interaction, even if you are working remotely from home.

- Ask questions – this will force you to listen intently. Do not hesitate to ask for clarification. Delivering work based on a wrong assumption is worse.
- Paraphrase your understanding and repeat it back to the person to ensure you have understood correctly.
- Take a genuine interest in what the person is saying. Most of the time, we wait for the other person to stop talking, so we can jump in with our thoughts.
- While someone is speaking, do not interrupt. Keep all your distractions (phone, email, etc.) away; no multi-tasking.

"Professionalism: It's NOT the job you DO, It's HOW you DO the job."

21

BEING A PROLIFIC PROFESSIONAL

"Your attitude, not your aptitude, will determine your altitude."- Zig Ziglar

Professionalism gets you noticed and puts you in line for leadership positions because you inspire trust, people enjoy interacting with you, and you always do your best.

Defined as "the conduct, aims, or qualities that characterize a professional person," professionalism is the cornerstone of any successful career – that means attitude and behavior. The former is reflected in external actions and reactions, and the latter in things like body language and mindset. Management experts repeat ad nauseam that having the right attitude and behavior is better than having all the right skills, which can be taught through training. Research suggests that having a positive attitude helps you cope better in stressful situations, making workdays easier. It cultivates patience and resilience.

Another benefit is motivation. An upbeat, hopeful comportment boosts team morale, improving the work environment and productivity; working in a hostile workplace can be extremely challenging. The benefits of acting professionally are personal and collective; you accelerate your career while increasing collaboration and productivity.

How to Cultivate a Good Attitude:

"Attitude" can be defined as the default patterns and responses. We all have them. Are yours supporting or deterring your professionalism and growth? Shifting those that do not serve to beneficial ones can be a lengthy process. However, if you put the following suggestions into practice, you will cultivate a new default mode in time.

- **Have a growth mindset:** Author Travis Bradberry explores how the two types of mindsets, growth and fixed, determine professional success. If you have a fixed mindset, you tend to believe that you cannot control or change yourself. A growth mindset will help you embrace every adversity as a learning opportunity.
- **Fail hard and bounce back:** Avoid indulging in feelings of helplessness. Learn to bounce back. Oprah Winfrey and Steven Spielberg were rejected and fired yet persevered. If they had fixed mindsets, they would not have taken a different route to success.
- **Show enthusiasm:** Be engaged and apply yourself. Dive into projects with interest and learn new skills eagerly. Try and get your team to approach situations similarly.
- **Be action-oriented:** Positive people do not become paralyzed by anxiety, challenges, and fear. They take action despite feeling overwhelmed. Their courage gets them noticed and builds their confidence.
- **Go the extra mile:** You may have heard of the famous example of Bruce Lee's pupil, who ran five miles despite thinking that he may die. The premise for pushing yourself is that if you are not getting better each day, you are stagnating or regressing. Of course, do not push yourself at the expense of your physical and mental health.
- **Demand the best from yourself:** People with a positive attitude expect results from themselves first and then from others. They are aware that they may fail occasionally, but this does not stop them from setting high standards for themselves. This trait is vital if you want to climb up the career ladder.

How to Cultivate Honorable Behavior?

In an article for *Chron*, Lynda Belcher lists behaviors that contribute to increased productivity and a healthy working environment. She points out that highly skilled workers are always welcome, but employers and employees prefer those with better behavior.

You can upgrade your professionalism by cultivating the following:

- **Respectfulness:** First and foremost, one needs to respect others – this means being polite to everyone, from clients to janitors. If you treat everyone with courtesy, conflict is often avoided and disagreements resolved in a mature manner.

- **Commitment:** If you do whatever it takes to reach your company's goals and continually develop new ideas, you will be seen as an asset. It sets you up for promotions and growth. Commitment and dedication are sought-after traits.
- **Kindness**: Helping others at work will get people to like you genuinely. Show consideration and understanding to everyone. It helps to remember people's names while interacting with them.
- **Pleasantness**: Everyone loves an agreeable, easy-to-work co-worker. Conversely, no one wants to be around someone moody, difficult, grim, uncooperative, and obstinate.
- **Integrity**: Standing firm in and operating from principles like honesty, reliability, trustworthiness, and honor is the cornerstone of positive behavior.

In addition to the above suggestions, the following hacks will help you cultivate a professional attitude and behavior:

Hack 61: Surefire Tips to Professional Conduct:

- **Be always on guard:** When you are in public, and especially at work, operate from the assumption that everyone is carefully watching your actions and reactions – because they are!
- **Don't get drawn into unprofessional behaviors:** Always speak well of yourself and others. Do not get drawn into gossip, badmouthing, and self-denigration.
  If people are engaging in such behavior around you, remove yourself from the situation.
- **Don't gripe to coworkers:** If you have a legitimate complaint, speak to those responsible, the management or HR.
- **Be neutral:** Be objective and unbiased at all times. Neutrality is easy when you remove yourself from the equation. If you are assembling a team, choose the most capable, not the most pliable.
  The same goes for solving problems. Your focus should be on finding the best solution, not about personally gaining from the situation.
- **Be open to all ideas:** Avoid being too attached to your ideas. Do not be envious or resentful if your colleagues come up with better ones. Aim to do what's best for the company.
- **Acknowledge everyone's contribution:** Even if you were the driving force behind a professional success, do not boast or take all the credit. Give credit where it is due, and make everyone on the team feel appreciated.

- **Spread some cheer:** Suggest and implement ways to boost morale. Team lunches and retreats help in creating an upbeat environment at work.
- **Maintain your professional comportment outside work:** Do not let your guard down or behave immaturely or inappropriately outside the workplace – this includes office parties, work functions, social media, etc. Drunken videos of yourself will undermine your professionalism.
- **Avoid the entitled mindset:** Regardless of how accomplished you are, stay humble and relevant. No one owes you a living; keep earning your stripes every day on the field. Do not rest on your laurels.

22

BEING VISIBLE

"You've got to find a way to make people know you're there."
-Nikki Giovanni

As kids, we all came across children who were more popular than we were. All the teachers knew them, and they got more attention. Even the brilliant but quiet kids often flew "under the radar." How important is visibility to your career? In one word: crucial.

People tend to blame favoritism when they lose positions that they were more qualified for to a more popular colleague, but that's somewhat unfair. Being visible takes effort and skill. This doesn't mean bragging about yourself every chance you get.

The key is to get noticed – in a subtle manner – for your attributes and contributions. The current work environment, especially corporate settings, is more competitive than ever. Working hard without promoting yourself is not a smart choice.

If key people are not aware of your potential, you will miss out on projects and promotions. Not only should the higher-ups know of you, but you also must know them. After all, it's all about connections.

How to Increase Your Visibility:

Professionals are showcasing their skills and expertise on platforms LinkedIn, writing blogs and ebooks, etc. Many feel uncomfortable, but it's critical to overcome shyness and hesitation. The following pointers will come in handy:

- **Speak up in meetings:** Read the agenda and go in with a plan. Have a set of ideas but respond to what others say. Although public speaking can be challenging, start by practicing in smaller groups with friends or trusted colleagues.
  You can also learn speaking skills online or join Toastmasters. Keep in mind that an engaging speaker knows the art of brevity and clarity.
- **Identify problems and offer fixes:** If you discover an issue that others have not seen, notify the manager, and take the initiative to fix it. Make sure that you tackle the problem effectively. Bonus points if you collaborate with a colleague but keep managers in the loop.
  For instance, if your colleagues are struggling with new software that you know, offer to teach people but seek permission from your boss first. Taking such an initiative makes life easier for others and you more visible.
- **Take on projects and tasks:** Offering to take up new projects will get you noticed, especially before being asked – this creates a good impression and helps others, especially if your team is overwhelmed. Don't fear if it isn't your typical project.
  Make a point to stretch yourself across departments and units. You will learn new skills, adapt to new environments, and expand your network.
- **Be open to feedback:** Nobody likes criticism, but one needs to listen to constructive input to improve; the key concept here is "constructive." Listening will always work in your favor. The key is to honestly consider whether the other person's point of view holds merit.
  It's equally important to note that you have to stand up for yourself. If you are right, then communicate that effectively and politely. If the criticism is on point, act quickly to show that you are serious about improving by setting micro deadlines, for example.

- **Be approachable:** Cultivate a friendly vibe. Smile, make eye contact, and chat with people in the hallways or break rooms. You can build meaningful connections by showing curiosity and being interested in other people and their work.
- **Volunteer:** Volunteering for leadership positions can be risky but also rewarding if you succeed. Follow Jim Rohn's rule of going above and beyond.
- **Find ways to showcase all your skills:** Say you're a graphic designer and a good writer. If you take it upon yourself to proofread texts while designing a publication, you save your company time and money. Your bosses will notice your efficiency and dedication.
- **Network and interact:** Take every opportunity to organize or attend events that will get you to interact with colleagues, especially in other departments and senior-level executives – this grants you broader visibility and aids in making connections beneficial for your growth.
- **Find a sponsor or mentor:** This is a senior person who uses their position in the organization to push you forward. They will help raise your profile, for example, by nominating you for choice projects or promotions. A mentor is a sounding board. They help you with the next move, offer advice, and probably teach you a thing or two.

So, to thrive, one needs to build a reputation and visibility by taking initiatives, forming collaborations, and creating connections.

Aside from the above ideas, consider the following hacks:

Hack 62: Bond with the Boss:

Building rapport with your superiors is critical to getting noticed. How can you accomplish that subtly and professionally?

- Ensure that you speak to your boss regularly. Meet with them at least once a week for about 10-15 minutes and bring value to these discussions. Keep meetings and conversations at work professional. However, as you start to build rapport with your boss, some personalization is fine. Avoid feigning interest in their life. Also, you don't necessarily have to share details of your personal life.
- Always go fully prepared to meetings and keep conversations crisp. If you have specific points to discuss, make notes, and plan ahead.
- Give your managers updates and keep them informed of any challenges. Seek their help if you require it.

- Present your proposals, solutions, and suggestions to your boss. This will not only bring a fresh pair of eyes to your ideas but also encourage collaboration.

Hack 63: Grow Your Network Offline:

How many people do you know outside of your team in your organization? Do you know at least two people in upper management, or are you essentially invisible? If you have no connections or exposure to management, then your chances of being noticed are next to none. You can fix this by:

- Make a concerted effort to meet people outside your immediate professional circle at your company and elsewhere. Attend networking events, conferences, conventions, forums, training seminars, etc. Research your company's hierarchy and identify people who can help your career. Connect with them on LinkedIn or in the workplace.
- At work, you can ask for a meeting if you have something specific to discuss or strike up a conversation with people who can help your career and managers from other teams. For example, break the ice in the cafeteria by commenting on the day's special. Be friendly but brief. Next time you see the person in the hallway, say hello.
Let the relationship develop organically. Avoid any manipulation. The key is to bond on mutual interests and have meaningful conversations.

Hack 64: Grow Your Network and Cachet Online.

- Use LinkedIn effectively. The platform is built to connect professionals. It helps you get noticed, get jobs, and also showcase your potential. It provides insight into the minds of employers and employees alike. It also gives indications of where your industry is headed and what you can learn to improve. Add your managers, colleagues, and competition as your connections. This will get you noticed for better jobs, collaborations, and projects.
- Build a strong online presence, especially if you are an expert or in the creative field. Recruiters today ask for LinkedIn profiles, and social media handles to get to know their candidates better. You can also create a personal website, which serves as a CV. It goes without saying that you need to keep all your social media accounts looking professional and wholesome.

- Even if you are not an expert or in a creative field, experts suggest getting creative with your resumes, like designing them on your Instagram or Facebook pages. You could also create a comprehensive resume using InDesign and supplement it with your LinkedIn profile.
- Showcase your industry knowledge by writing articles and informative posts. Out of sight is out of mind, so ensure that you post regularly. Next time your manager is looking for someone to handle a challenging project on whose theme you write about regularly on social media, they may consider you for the role.

"Don't worry about being successful. Work toward being significant and the success will naturally follow."
- Oprah Winfrey

23

DEVELOP AN ENTREPRENEURIAL MINDSET

"Those who are crazy enough to think they can change the world usually do."
- Steve Jobs

The term "entrepreneur" brings to mind high-flying business leaders and innovators – people with superior vision, abilities, resourcefulness, courage, and appetites for risk. Indeed, such individuals innately possess traits that support their journeys through life, both in success and failure, since resilience is also required.

Most people do not feel they have "what it takes" to be entrepreneurs, so they settle. However, Sorin V. Chiriac clarifies that entrepreneurs are not special humans, and the entrepreneur's traits can be developed. Whether you wish to start your own business or accelerate your career, cultivating an entrepreneurial mindset would be beneficial.

When you see yourself as the CEO of your life, you become more driven and productive. You are less likely to be dragged from one dead-end job to another. You realize that it's up to you to take charge of your career, make the best choices, and follow through every day. Ultimately, it makes you relentless when it comes to your success.

How to Cultivate an Entrepreneurial Mindset:

Whether you are new to the workforce or a seasoned professional, it's never too early or late to implement the following:

- Believe that anything is possible. You cannot bring anything to fruition unless you believe that it's achievable. By having confidence in your plan, you train your mind to find solutions to your problems quickly. Also, be solution-oriented. Some people are problem-oriented – unconsciously looking for reasons why something cannot be done – while others look for ways to accomplish it. Go after the things you want using the resources at hand.
- Appreciate your accomplishments, no matter how small they are. Having this outlook is imperative when you face setbacks and need to be resilient. It also teaches you to be patient. Learn to delegate. You can't do it all by yourself. Surround yourself with people who will contribute to your success and growth.
- Work with the best. Avoid being the smartest one in the room. Interact and collaborate with people with whom you disagree and who challenge you to do better. They will help you stay motivated and improve consistently. Focus on your work, not on what others are doing. The grass will always appear greener on the other side. It is critical to be aware of your competition and remain one step ahead. However, it is not wise to spend copious amounts of money and time monitoring or copying your competitors. Invest in building a unique approach. Individuality and innovation set you apart.
- Take action and be decisive. While it's essential to develop an idea fully before taking action, do not sit on it too long. Ideas are successful only when they hit the market at the right moment. When you have an idea, patent it, and get to work.
- Treat every day as a new beginning. Even when things are tough, realize that you have the power to turn the situation around tomorrow. Take responsibility. While it is unrealistic to believe that you can control everything, it is also foolish to think that you have no control over anything; it is also a convenient excuse not to push yourself. Consider challenges a blessing and learn from them.

- Avoid the blame game and the martyr mindset. If you believe that nobody values you, or that you're not good enough, or that everyone is taking advantage of you, then you are bound to experience that until the end of your days. Only you can change your life.
- Combine idealism and pragmatism. If you have a dream about how the world should be, turn it into a vision and a goal. Dedicate your skills and resources to realize that dream. If you dream about a pollution-free planet, consider environmental activism or building recycling plants.
- Yes, I can! If you are stuck in patterns of disbelief, negativity, and pessimism, replace every negative thought with a positive one by saying, "I can do it," rather than "I cannot."

Even if you never own a business, you can see yourself as your 'entrepreneurial project.' To stay ahead and relevant in the job market, you must reinvent yourself constantly.

The entrepreneurial mindset will help you identify problems, find solutions, think strategically, act purposefully, have a vision, and seek innovation.

Hack 65: Tips on How to Think Like an Entrepreneur:

- Let your passion guide you. If you don't love your work, then it's time to explore other opportunities. Even if you are not able to change jobs, transfer to another department, reimagine and expand your role.
- Use all resources at your disposal. This can take many forms, like retraining, brainstorming with people with novel perspectives, using new software, etc. If you are running a business, this will take your business to new levels; if you are an employee, your employability and value will increase.
- Find your unique selling proposition. All entrepreneurs and businesses have something that sets them apart. Identify your strengths and leverage them to become a sought-after expert.
- Do not tolerate mediocrity in yourself or others. If you're an employee, ensure that you do not produce poor or mediocre work. If you are a manager, set a high standard for everyone, including yourself.
- Take calculated risks. Whether you are an employer or employee, you need to take risks to grow without acting impulsively or recklessly. Apply for challenging roles outside your comfort zone. Be smart about it, and take risks that can yield high returns.

- Be goal-oriented. Set attainable short-term and long-term goals and work diligently toward them. If you get stuck, brainstorm with trusted and like-minded colleagues and come up with new approaches.
- Take initiatives. Entrepreneurs are self-starters. They challenge the status quo by coming up with creative solutions. Being self-motivated and self-directed will set you apart as a leader, not a follower.
- Go beyond your pay. Offer more value for the money by "going above and beyond" – this is especially useful when starting a new company or career. See this as an investment in yourself because it helps you become the best you can be and also be indispensable. One approach you can use is asking yourself, "If I were the owner of this firm, how would I solve the problem?"
- Manage your time and focus. Avoid distractions as much as possible, putting time into things that will propel you, like attending networking events rather than chilling with Netflix every night.
- Be adaptable and future-oriented. Like inventors, when entrepreneurs see a problem, they see an opportunity to develop a solution they can market. They work according to a plan but remain flexible. Adapting to change easily will make you future-oriented rather than stuck in the past.

24

FUTURE-PROOFING YOURSELF

"Unlearning is the single most important skill for the 21st century. Ignore at your own peril."
– Ravi Kummar

The world is moving ahead at a dizzying pace. The adage, "Change is the only constant," has never been more apropos. Predictions like "Humans will lose their jobs to machines soon" indicate that we must be prepared to meet the market's requirements.

An article on Singularity University's blog, describing tech trends and their exponential rise, points out that it took the mobile phone 12 years to reach 50 million; Pokémon Go took 19 days to get 50 million users.

Such applications grow so rapidly because they are built on existing technology. It's easy to deliver new features and products to the palms of millions of users.

Companies must keep reinventing themselves to keep up with the trends. If you want to thrive in this economy, can you afford not to future-proof yourself?

Five Trends That Will Define the Future:

The following areas are growing exponentially and influencing more and more business operations. While reading them, think of the ones that excite you and the steps you need to take to achieve those goals.

- **Artificial Intelligence:** AI is growing by leaps and bounds, becoming cheaper and more accessible. Many companies use it to their advantage, and many will follow.

- **Augmented and Virtual Reality:** AR and VR are rapidly improving and used in different areas like medicine, education, architecture, gaming, etc. We should expect to see more of this technology across sectors.
- **Autonomous vehicles:** From Ford to Tesla, everyone is in the game. It is predicted that this innovation will rapidly expand by 2027 and profoundly impact our lives.
- **Data Science**: LinkedIn listed Data Scientist as the fastest-growing job. The field will continue to be a critical driver of the global economy.
- **Robotics:** The technology is becoming affordable and efficient. Collaborative robots are already working with humans, assisting with tasks like monitoring inventories, helping customers, medicine, even treating conditions like autism.

How to Future-Proof Your Career:

You don't have to be a "techie" to future-proof yourself, as one might infer from the above list. There are many things you can do to thrive in a changing world.

- **Cultivate and enhance your soft skills:** While the world is speeding toward automation, the World Economic Forum and leaders such as Sheryl Sandberg and Eric Schmidt place more importance on soft rather than hard skills in today's job market.
  - **Curiosity:** Organizations prefer curious candidates because they are proactive in educating themselves. They require clarity about the tasks they are assigned, so they tend to perform them better.
  - **Confidence:** Research shows that bright candidates recruited from colleges often possess low confidence. Millennials and GenZ suffer from the imposter syndrome – this hinders their performance. You need to produce quality work to thrive; if you try to "fake it until you make it," you will be caught out eventually. The only way to develop true confidence is by developing your skills. Evaluate yourself honestly and work towards fixing your shortcomings instead of feeling sorry for yourself.
  - **Creative thinking:** This is vastly different from providing solutions to problems. Employers prefer employees who think outside the box and innovate.

As such, creative professionals have an advantage. Nurture your creativity by generating ideas or picking up a hobby.
- **People skills:** Patience, helpfulness, thoughtfulness, humor, friendliness, etc. You will be selected over candidates with exceptional knowledge and below-par people skills if you possess great people skills.
- **Leadership and boldness**: Most employees wait passively for instructions. Instead, be self-driven, bold, and confident. Attend leadership programs or take classes to hone your potential.
- **Flexibility.** Being adaptable and open to change is essential, both in terms of your personality and skillset. Take any opportunity to explore new ways of doing things and do not resist change; see it as an opportunity to grow.

- **Be proactive**: Keep abreast of politics, technology, and the economy so you can anticipate and adapt. For example, take classes on the tech that your company wants to adopt. Everyone needs to upgrade to stay relevant, so beat others to the punch.
- **Think laterally and explore shifting economies**: Identify roles in overlooked sectors that may align with your interests. For example, a nurse with business acumen may conceive an app-based business that provides nursing services on short notice.
- **Use your words:** Be vocal about your aspirations with HR and management. Show that you are open to growth and other options.
- **Get advice and inspiration**: Of course, it's not easy to have a personal "board of advisors and mentors," especially at the beginning of your career.
You can start with online communities, coaches, motivational speakers, and TED Talks to make the right decisions and find support.

Machines may render some jobs redundant but cannot replace the human connection. It is essential to emphasize that humans are indispensable. That said, today is a good day to begin future-proofing your career with the following hacks:

Hack 66: Be Tech-Savvy:

No matter which role you're in, learn as much as you can. Up-to-date tech skills are beneficial regardless of whether you change jobs or not.

Hack 67: Develop Transferable Skills and Core Competencies:

Things like leadership, communication, creativity, and people skills are sought-after across domains. The more you have, the greater your advantage.

Hack 68: Maintain a Success Journal:

This will come in handy when you ask for a promotion or need to showcase your achievements to a potential employer. It also affirms your strengths and builds your confidence and self-esteem.

Hack 69: Unlearn:

Keep up with the times and let go of obsolete approaches, replacing them with new ones. For instance, if you're a writer, learn about inclusive language so you can leave out outdated, offensive terms from your copy.

Hack 70: Keep Evaluating and Investing in Yourself:

Ask, "What can I do to make myself indispensable or carve out a new path, even within the same company?" For example, when a company automates a few tasks, employees have more time on their hands. Put this time to use by taking up new responsibilities. The chances of you being laid off are lower and getting a promotion higher. It will also give you experience in new areas. Use a percentage of your income to upskill or invest in your business, like buying software that will open up new income streams.

Hack 71: Become a Trouble-Shooter:

Strive to become the company's go-to person when it comes to coming up with solutions – this will make you an invaluable asset.

Hack 72: Become a Mediator:

To avoid conflict, many people tolerate negative situations in the workplace, leaving things to fester. Even if you are not in HR, you can make yourself valuable by mediating. Be objective but also mindful about doing the right thing. Look at the situation from different perspectives to arrive at a comprehensive solution acceptable to all sides.

TAKE CHARGE OF YOUR HEALTH AND WELL-BEING
A fit body leads to a calm mind, and this is all you need.

"To ensure good health: eat lightly, breathe deeply, live moderately, cultivate cheerfulness, and maintain an interest in life."
-William Londen

25

ENVIRONMENTAL POLLUTION AND TOXICITY

"In our world, these harmful micro-organisms and an endless list of toxic chemicals consistently assault our immune system.
Coupled with these assaults are the daily stresses of life and their deleterious effects upon us." – David Wolfe

"The first wealth is health." Ralph Waldo Emerson emphasized that health and wellness are the cornerstones of thriving above self-actualization, success, career, and money. It is my firm belief that the extent of illness and malaise that we experience in the world today is a direct result of environmental pollution and toxicity.

The issue needs to be addressed collectively, like in 2019, when millions took to the streets demanding that world leaders address climate change. We must defend against it on an individual level as if our lives depended on it because they do! We begin this section of the book with broader issues, not to discourage but empower you with information, outlining a realistic, practical plan to take charge of your health and well-being despite the toxic soup.

Understanding Pollution and Toxicity:

Toxicity is the degree to which a chemical, biological, physical, or energetic substance can damage an organism through ingestion, inhalation, or transdermal contact. The exposure we have the least control over is pollution – the presence or introduction of damaging materials and conditions into the natural environment due to human activity.

Here, we look at factors that can adversely affect our health, especially if we live in urban or industrial areas.

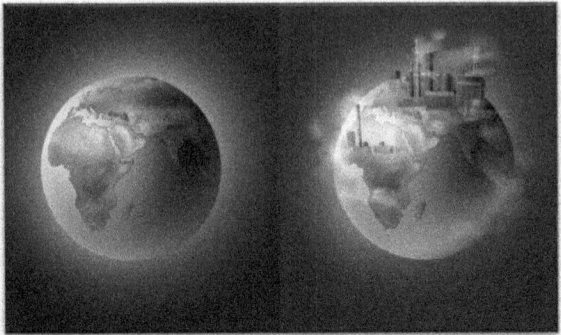

- **Water and thermal pollution:** The release of harmful chemicals, microorganisms, and energy (radioactivity and heat) into oceans, lakes, and rivers.
- **Air pollution:** Pollutants emitted into the atmosphere include gases and biological molecules.
- **Land and soil pollution:** The destruction or decline in the quality of the earth's land in terms of use, landscape, and ability to support life.
- **EMF pollution:** Electric and magnetic fields (EMFs), also referred to as "radiation," is produced by electricity by power lines, cell phones, microwaves, etc.
- **Noise pollution:** The noise produced by traffic, industry, and human activity impacts health and well-being because people cannot relax or sleep.
- **Light pollution:** The lengthened and excessive use of artificial lights upsets the natural cycles of wildlife and humans.
- **Heavy metals:** While the body needs small amounts of some heavy metals (e.g., zinc, copper, iron, manganese), heavy metal toxicity is the excessive build-up of metals like mercury, aluminum, lead, arsenic, and cadmium in the body. Some industries are hotbeds for occupational exposure (battery and thermometer production, welding, soldering, incandescent lights, x-ray machines, etc.). However, everyone is exposed daily to air or water pollution, foods, medicines, cookware, paints, insecticides, herbicides, pesticides, etc. Common effects include headaches, irritability, mood swings; vision, neurological and gastrointestinal problems; reproductive, lungs, kidneys, brain damage; skin changes; cancer. Diagnosis involves blood, urine, kidney, and liver function tests.

Acute heavy metal poisoning is treated with chelating agents, which bind to the metal and are excreted in the urine.
- **Mold:** Mold is fungi that bloom in dampness. Aspergillus, Alternaria, Acremonium, Cladosporium, Dreschslera, Epicoccum, Penicillium, Stachybotrys, and Trichoderma are common indoor species with detrimental effects, like respiratory diseases, fatigue, anxiety, headaches, nosebleeds, weakened muscles, restless legs, lightheadedness, allergies, autoimmune disorders, inflammation and more.

Our Collective Responsibility:

Environmental pollution is an incurable disease:
it can only be prevented.
- Barry Commoner

In addition to applying political pressure, responsibility rests on all of us to do our part. Consider the following actions:

- **Solar power:** The cost of solar panels is dropping every year. Consider generating electricity to the extent you can afford to do so.
- **Public transport:** Walk, cycle, or use public transport as often as possible, improving your health at the same time.
- **Clean water:** Conserve clean water and consider rainwater harvesting at home. You can also join NGOs and social clubs that set up clean drinking water plants for poor communities.
- **Vote with your wallet:** The less we support harmful industries and products, the more incentivized industry leaders will feel to produce cleaner solutions.

On a personal level, the following hacks will help you reduce your exposure to environmental pollutants and toxins:

Hack 73: Beware of What You Put into Your Body:

Consume chemical-free food. Buy fresh and organic as often as possible. Wash your vegetables and fruits using hot water with salt and turmeric. With affordable hydroponics kits, you can grow greens and vegetables at home.

Drink clean water that is free of fluoride, which is hazardous and can even cause toxicity. Use natural cosmetic/hygiene products; things like lotions contain harmful substances like parabens, which are absorbed into your skin, the largest organ in the body.

Hack 74: Cleanse and Detoxify:

Since toxins have a long-lasting impact, it is essential not only to limit exposure but also to detoxify. While chelation is a medical treatment for heavy metal poisoning, there are many over-the-counter products and home remedies that can help.

- **Cleanse:** Certain herbs, which are not part of the normal diet, help in detoxification. There are countless formulations on the market for specific organs and purposes, but the main ones are burdock root, sarsaparilla, dandelion, mullein, bromelain, papain, elderberry, and cilantro.
- **Foods:** Increasing intake of cruciferous vegetables, lemon, green tea, garlic, turmeric, chlorella, beets, blueberries, and tomatoes boosts the body's ability to eliminate toxins.
- **Water:** Drinking plenty of water helps flush our toxins daily.
- **Sweat:** Sweat expedites the removal of toxins. Make sure to continuously wipe your skin so as not to reabsorb the toxins. Also, make sure there are no lotions to inhibit the elimination.
- **Sleep:** A good night's sleep allows your brain to eliminate toxins.

Hack 75: Mold Exposure:

Consider a urine mycotoxin screen if you think you've been exposed. The following things will help you speed up recovery:

- **Avoid moldy foods:** According to Dave Asprey, you can speed up recovery by avoiding moldy foods: all grains except white rice; corn, beans, oats, peanuts, cottonseed; cheese; bread; pork (unless pastured); aged meats; all alcohol, but wine and beer are the worst; coffee and chocolate (unless mold-tested); dried fruit; Brazil nuts; pistachios; chili, pre-ground black pepper, and other spices.
- **Detox therapies:** Infrared saunas, 24-hour fasting, cryotherapy or ice baths, red light therapy, acupuncture, and intravenous vitamin C or glutathione can accelerate recovery.

26

HOLISTIC HEALTH

"He who has health has hope, and he who has hope has everything." – Thomas Carlyle

The World Health Organization defines health as "complete physical, mental, and social well-being, not merely the absence of disease or infirmity." Also referred to as "holistic," this is a state where optimal health and wellness are achieved without the need for artificial substances and invasive procedures.

Understanding Holistic Living:

Rooted in the Greek word *holos*, which means total, the holistic approach considers the whole person, in contrast to modern medicine, which generally alleviates symptoms rather than cures the underlying condition. It considers everything that affects a person's life, physical, emotional, mental, and spiritual. Since these factors are inextricably linked, their balance or imbalance determines one's life trajectory.

Let's gain a better understanding:

- **Physical health:** This means being free of chronic conditions as well as feeling strong and vital. Nutrition, exercise, and sleep are the cornerstones of physical health.
- **Emotional and mental well-being:** You cannot stay physically healthy for long if you are in emotional and mental distress. Anxiety, stress, and unhappiness flood the body with detrimental hormones.

If left unchecked, they create health issues. Not everyone bounces back from painful experiences or adapts to change easily.

While love and patience from other people help, each person must find healthy ways to return to emotional and mental balance. For example, going for a run when stressed rather than chain-smoking.

- **Spiritual wellness:** Many factors define spirituality, religious faith, beliefs, and values. Ultimately, it boils down to how you see yourself in the world: Are you alone in life and separated from the Creator? Or do you feel connected to the universe and the larger picture? The first perspective can create feelings of emptiness and meaninglessness, leading to depression, alienation, and existential despair. The second anchors your life with meaning and purpose.

The Keys to Holistic Living:

In this section of the book, we present the keys to health and wellness. Sleep, exercise, and hydration are fundamental. However, as the famous Ayurvedic saying goes, "Everything – health and sickness starts in the gut." Diet is of primary importance, but it's not only what you put in your stomach but also how much and when. Across centuries and cultures, fasting was said to have significant health benefits. While most modern doctors disagree, in recent years, scientists have discovered its benefits. In addition, we highlight breathwork and meditation. A mindfulness practice will help you connect to yourself and your Creator. The techniques are countless.

Thriving in mind and body is within reach. There has never been a time in history when more healing and rebalancing modalities have been so widely available. Acupuncture, reflexology, naturopathy, massage, Reiki, psychotherapy, hypnosis, the list is endless.

Although we will delve into the particulars in the next chapters, the following hack serves as the foundation for your journey to achieving or optimizing a holistic lifestyle.

Hack 76: Health and Wellness Journal:

To take charge of your health and wellness, you need to be aware of your patterns to adjust them. The process involves four steps:

Step 1: Track your daily activities without trying to change your habits. Simply record the following for at least one week:

- o The number of sleep-hours and wake-up times.
- o Mealtimes and the food you consume – the percentage of fruits, vegetables, protein, and carbohydrates.

- How much water do you drink per day?
- How much physical exercise do you get per day?
- How many unhealthy substances do you consume and in what quantities – alcohol, cigarettes, etc.?
- How many over-the-counter medications do you use, like painkillers and sleep aids?
- Height, weight, and Body Mass Index [BMI].
- How many hours of negative media do you consume?
- How much time do you dedicate to a mindfulness practice like meditation, prayer, and introspection?
- How much time do you spend with your loved ones?
- How much time do you spend amidst nature?
- How much time do you spend doing something that you love, like art or playing music?

Step 2: Analyze the information. Once you've gathered enough data, calculate the averages.

Step 3: Identify the things you need to change. Note all the things that do not contribute to optimum health and divide them into two lists. The first list should include those you can shift fairly easily. For example, if you are not drinking enough water, bring a water bottle everywhere you go. The second list should include matters that require professional help. For example, if you are taking painkillers for headaches often, find out what is causing the problem by seeing a health practitioner.

Step 4: Take action. Eliminating all unhealthy habits will take time, but "a journey of a thousand miles begins with the first step." To stay motivated, start with a couple of things that you can change easily, like increasing your water intake. Simultaneously, pick a more severe concern, like the recurring headaches, and get to the root of the problem.

"About eighty percent of the food on shelves of supermarkets today didn't exist 100 years ago."
— Dr. Larry McCleary

27

DIET

"Let food be thy medicine and medicine be thy food."
- Hippocrates

According to the World Health Organization, a healthy diet ensures that one consumes enough nutrients to prevent malnutrition; it should not lead to diabetes, stroke, hypertension, heart disease, obesity, and other diet-related conditions.

In other words, it's critical to eat the right foods in the right amounts.

In addition, the diet should be tailored to age, gender, lifestyle, and physical activity. Cultural context and local foods also play a role. Urbanization and the increased availability of processed foods make it difficult for many to maintain a healthy diet; hungry, rushed, and stressed people on the move reach for food high in fats, sugars, and sodium that is almost always low in nutrients.

They may skip fruits, vegetables, and other dietary fibers. That said, except for people who truly do not have access to nutritious food due to dire socioeconomic conditions, for the rest of us, it is a choice regardless of our excuses!

Start with the Basics:

When we make a poor diet habitual, we risk our health and well-being. The following modifications can help you get on the right track fairly quickly and easily:

- **Choose fresh and natural:** Avoid anything that comes out of a box like frozen entrees, canned vegetables, legumes, soups, etc. Processed foods are full of unhealthy additives and preservatives.
  If you look at the list of ingredients, you will see a list of chemicals. As a rule of thumb, if you don't know what it is and cannot pronounce it, don't consume it.
- **Increase plant-based food:** A healthy diet is rich in fruits, vegetables, legumes, nuts, and whole grains. You need to have at least 400 grams of vegetables per day, excluding starchy vegetables. Include vegetables in your meals; this can't be said enough. Consume fresh fruits or raw vegetables as snacks. Make it a point to eat produce that is local and in season.
- **Reduce trans fats:** Prevent unhealthy weight gain and related health conditions by consuming less than 30% of fat in your total energy intake and eliminating industrially processed fats. This means cutting down on things like pizza, cookies, and pies.
- **Limit sugar:** Sugar intake must be less than 12 teaspoons for a person with a healthy body weight consuming at least 2000 calories a day. Cutting down can be a challenge if you have a sweet tooth. Start by not drinking it in carbonated drinks, flavored milk, and ready-to-drink coffees. Also, replace sweets with healthy alternatives. For example, every time you feel like dessert, whip up a fresh fruit bowl instead.
- **Limit fried food:** Try to steam, boil, or broil your food as opposed to frying. If you don't think you can do without fried food, buy an air-fryer; it uses the tiniest amount of oil to replicate the taste and texture.
- **Limit salt:** Cut down on salt used in cooking and replace it with a high-quality natural salt, like Himalayan pink, which is packed with around 84 minerals with great health benefits. Eliminate chips and processed snacks because they come with high salt content and contribute to conditions like hypertension.

If you are eating a very unhealthy diet at the moment, making the switch to healthier options might be challenging at first. Rest assured that your body will switch off cravings for fats, sugars, and salt if you stay the course. In fact, at some point, you will likely develop an aversion to very unhealthy foods and feel unwell when you eat them.

When the body is back in balance, its wisdom will guide you. However, if your goal is to address specific concerns like weight loss, you can choose a diet that fits your needs.

Choosing the Right Diet:

> *When diet is wrong, medicine is of no use.*
> *When diet is correct, medicine is of no need.*
> *-Ayurvedic Proverb*

Every day we hear about a new diet. There are certainly enough fads out there to confuse people. The reality is that customizing your diet can help you achieve specific health goals, like weight loss and healthy cholesterol levels. Since it's impossible to list every diet here, we limit the following list to those popular today – with the caveat that if you are tackling a specific health concern, seek professional advice.

- **The Atkins Diet:** Consult a doctor before adopting a diet like Atkins. It focuses on controlling the levels of insulin and reduces the risk of diabetes. It is low on carbohydrates and helps with weight loss as it works on the principle of ketosis. The foods consumed are fiber-rich vegetables like broccoli, asparagus, greens, and fruits low in sugar, like berries and citrus. There is an emphasis on whole grains, nuts, avocados, and olive oil, plant-based fats. Coffee and green tea are allowed.
- **The Ketogenic Diet:** It makes use of a metabolic process called ketosis, wherein the body burns its stored fats when it does not have enough glucose for energy. It eliminates carbohydrates and is often very high in fat, although variants suit different needs. It may result in quick weight loss. The Keto Diet is known to have many health benefits and risks. Therefore, consult your doctor.
- **The Mediterranean Diet:** One of the healthiest diets has its roots in southern Europe, Greece, and Italy. Its focus is plant-based foods, like fruits, nuts, beans, whole grains, and olive oil. It also includes a significant amount of fish, poultry, eggs, and wine. One-third is comprised of healthy fats. The Mediterranean Diet has been studied extensively, and there is credible research that it increases the quality of life and reduces the risk of many diseases.

- **The Vegan Diet:** Veganism is more than a diet; it's a way of life that people adopt for more than health, ethical, and environmental reasons. They believe that modern farming methods are bad for the planet and unsustainable in the long term.

  This diet is based on the premise that if everyone ate plant-based food, the environment would benefit, animals would suffer less, more food would be produced, and people would generally enjoy better physical and mental health.

  Vegans do not eat anything animal-based – meat, eggs, dairy, even honey. They eat only plant-based foods like vegetables, fruits, whole grains, legumes, tofu, mushrooms, nuts, and seeds.
- **Other diets:** In addition to the above, diets like the Paleo Diet (very similar to Atkins but more strict), the Dukan Diet, and the Ultra Low-Fat Diet also exist. Different diets work for different people, and you should pick one that suits your lifestyle, goals, and needs.
- **Professional advice:** When tackling a specific health concern, always seek professional advice. Food is medicine, so what you put into your body really matters.

If you are serious about health and longevity, you must eat only healthy food and eliminate processed food altogether. Here are a few hacks:

Hack 77: Out of Sight, Out of Mouth:

The first thing you need to do is get rid of all unhealthy foods from your pantry and desk at work. If you can't reach for it, you won't eat it.

Hack 78: Prepare Healthy Snacks Ahead of Time:

We all like to munch on chips and cookies in front of the TV. The way around this is to prepare healthy snacks ahead of time. For example, pre-cut carrots and celery sticks and sprinkle them with lemon juice and a bit of Himalayan salt – this way, you can satisfy your craving for a savory snack while doing something good for your body. Or reach for some seaweed!

Hack 79: Consume Healthy Fats:

Your mother was right; ghee is good for you. Eat lots of healthy fats like avocadoes, nuts, coconut, coconut oil, olives, olive oil, etc. Not only will these do wonders for your body, but they are also very satisfying.

Don't overdo it if you are trying to lose weight or consider a diet like Keto that incorporates them in a way that helps you lose weight.

Hack 80: Eat Local and Seasonal:

Your grandmother's advice was sound: Whatever grows around you is good for you. Eat lots of local and seasonal produce instead of packed food. Local and seasonal produce is less likely to be picked off the tree unripe. It is full of nutrients you need based on the climate and geography.

Hack 81: Swap Refined Carbs for Legumes and Whole Grains:

Instead of pasta, eat dhal. Serve your fish or meat with a side of beans. The market is full of healthy and ancient grains from all over the world, like quinoa, millet, barley, bulgur, buckwheat, and amaranth. Some are actually superfoods. Have fun exploring new flavors and recipes.

Hack 82: Fast:

Practice some form of fasting regularly, time-restricted eating (or intermittent fasting). Fasting is so vital that it is discussed at length in a dedicated chapter.

"The road to health is paved with good intestines!"
— Sherry A. Rogers

28

GUT HEALTH

"All disease starts in the gut." – Hippocrates

Did you know that your gut is one of the most critical organs in your body? And that as much as 70% of your immune system resides there? We think of the digestive system as the 'mill' where food is broken down so that the bloodstream can absorb it as nutrients. When it isn't in good shape, your body won't receive the necessary nourishment. Worse still, it will spread harmful substances throughout your system. Modern science is proving what ancient physicians knew – that health and well-being are inextricably linked to the gut. You are what you eat, after all.

Understanding the Role of the Gut:

Gut health depends on the balance of microorganisms that live in the digestive tract – the trillions of bacteria, yeasts, and viruses called the "gut microbiome" or "gut flora."

Many are beneficial, some essential, and others harmful, especially when they multiply. The gut is thought to be the seat of emotion. Anger, anxiety, sadness, joy, and happiness 'arise' in the gut, sending signals to the brain – this has been encoded in language with expressions like "gut instinct," "gut reaction," or "gut-wrenching."

Scientists from Institut Pasteur, Inserm, and CNRS have shown that an imbalance in gut bacteria can reduce certain metabolites, resulting in depressive behaviors. It's no surprise considering that 70% of serotonin is produced in the gut. Serotonin has many functions, but people call it "the happy chemical." The gut is also referred to as the "second brain" because it communicates with the brain through nerves and hormones.

When microbiome balance is disrupted by stress, illness, or poor diet, it can result in digestive problems, obesity, diabetes, irritable bowel syndrome, celiac disease, colitis, and – surprisingly perhaps – dementia, Alzheimer's, Parkinson's, and multiple sclerosis. The gut and the brain are closely connected, communicating through a system known as "the gut-brain axis," influencing digestion, appetite, and cravings. This axis comprises brain cells (neurons), hormones, and proteins that allow the brain to send messages to the gut and vice versa. The microbiome influences brain activity through the vagus nerve, which snakes through the body, linking internal organs to the brainstem. Through this connection, harmful pathogens and abnormal proteins can be transmitted to the brain.

Maintaining Gut Health:

It stands to reason that the primary factor of gut health would be diet; however, there are many others.

- **Probiotics:** They support a healthy microbiome, preventing gut inflammation and intestinal problems. Some people take supplements to increase beneficial bacteria, but this can be achieved naturally by including fermented foods in your diet (e.g., fermented vegetables, kefir, probiotic yogurt, kimchi, kombucha, miso, sauerkraut, tempeh).
- **Prebiotic fiber:** Probiotics feed on non-digestible carbohydrates called "prebiotics," encouraging beneficial bacteria to multiply. To enhance gut health, consume more of the following foods: asparagus, plantains, sweet potato, chicory, garlic, Jerusalem artichoke, onions, and whole grains.
- **Sugar and sweeteners:** These cause gut dysbiosis, an imbalance of microbes that affect the brain and behavior. Aspartame increases bacterial strains linked to metabolic disease, a group of conditions that increase the risk of diabetes and heart disease.

- **Stress:** Even short-term psychological and environmental stress (extreme heat, cold, or noise), sleep deprivation, and disruption of the circadian rhythm can disrupt flora balance.
- **Antibiotics.** They save millions of lives from infections by killing harmful bacteria or stopping them from multiplying. However, they can also destroy as much as 90% of the good bacteria in the gut.

Maintaining or restoring gut health is crucial to your health and well-being. While the following suggestions should never replace diagnosis and treatment by a qualified professional, they will help you get started:

Hack 83: Signs of an Unhealthy Gut:

Many symptoms, seemingly unrelated to the gut, may indicate an imbalance. These are common ways that an unhealthy gut manifests:

- **Digestive issues, food intolerances:** A healthy gut has less difficulty processing food and eliminating waste. Upset stomach, gas, bloating, constipation, diarrhea, heartburn, and nausea can be signs of an imbalance. There is also evidence that food allergies may be related to gut health.
- **Skin problems:** Gut inflammation increases the "leaking" of certain proteins into the body that irritate the skin and cause skin conditions like eczema.
- **Sugar cravings:** Processed foods and added sugars can decrease good bacteria, increasing sugar cravings that damage the gut further. High amounts of refined sugars lead to inflammation, a precursor to many diseases, including cancer.
- **Unexplained weight changes:** Gaining or losing weight without modifying diet or exercise habits may indicate that the gut does not absorb nutrients, regulate blood sugar, or store fat properly. Weight loss may be caused by small intestinal bacterial overgrowth (SIBO) and weight gain by insulin resistance or the urge to overeat due to decreased nutrient absorption.
- **Sleep disruptions:** Most of the body's serotonin, a hormone that affects mood and sleep, is produced in the gut. Gut damage can impair one's ability to sleep well, even increase the risk for fibromyalgia.
- **Chronic fatigue:** Certain biomarkers in gut bacteria have been linked to Chronic Fatigue Syndrome. They trigger inflammation, affect the central nervous and immune systems, causing tiredness, pain, poor concentration, memory loss, etc.

- **Autoimmune conditions:** An unhealthy gut increases systemic inflammation and disrupts the immune system, leading to autoimmune disorders, where the body attacks itself rather than harmful invaders.

Hack 84: Restore Gut Flora When Taking Antibiotics:

Restore proper digestion and absorption using probiotics with a high number of colony-forming units (CFUs) and digestive enzymes.

Hack 85: Tips for Gut Health:

Although we have covered these already, the following list can serve as an easy reference:

- Consume a whole-food, plant-based diet rich in fruits, vegetables, fermented foods, and nuts (especially almonds).
- Sleep, rest, and de-stress.
- Limit alcohol.
- Avoid artificial sweeteners, refined sugars, processed foods, farmed fish and meat, and gluten.

29

METABOLISM

"Metabolism is a basic characteristic of living systems. We have, as it were, a machine composed of fuel spending itself continually and yet maintaining itself."
– Ludwig von Bertalanffy

Metabolism is the physiological process of converting food into energy and eliminating waste. Since good metabolism is a vital factor in health, we will look at it closely and suggest ways to optimize it.

Understanding Metabolism:

There are two parts to metabolism:

- Catabolism is the process of breaking down large molecules into simpler ones.
- Anabolism builds up compounds such as proteins, carbohydrates, lipids, and nucleic acids. In short, catabolism releases energy, and anabolism consumes it.

The following factors affect this important physiological process:

- **Metabolic flexibility:** Our ancient ancestors often went for days without food but survived because of what is known as "metabolic flexibility." When no external source of fuel is available, the body burns stored fat or glucose. The ability to switch between carbohydrate metabolism and fat oxidation is called metabolic flexibility. In modern times, food is abundant for most people.

Since glucose is the easiest fuel source, the body gets used to burning glucose instead of fat. As a result, the body can forget how to burn fat. Therefore, when we don't eat regularly, we experience dizziness, weakness, shaky hands, and even fainting despite having plenty of stored fat in our bodies. Overconsumption of glucose-rich food and lack of adequate physical exercise seems to be at the root of severe conditions like insulin resistance, type-II diabetes, and cardiovascular diseases. If you get the urge to eat every few hours, it may mean that you have lost the ability to burn fat.

- **Basal Metabolic Rate:** A significant indicator of health is a high BMR – this refers to the number of calories the body requires to accomplish its basic functions. Did you know that you burn calories at rest for life-sustaining functions like breathing, circulation, nutrient processing, and cell production? Whether your goal is to lose body fat, gain muscle, or maintain weight, knowing your BMR can help you attain your goals.

- **Circadian rhythm and light:** Often referred to as the "body clock," the circadian rhythm is a natural cycle that tells the body when to sleep, rise, and eat, regulating many physiological processes. According to research by Satchin Panda, a circadian biologist at the Salk Institute for Biological Studies, everything in the human body – every hormone, chemical, and enzyme – is pre-programmed to peak at a specific time of the day and slow down at other times.
These mechanisms primarily respond to light and darkness in the organism's environment.

As such, the second factor to good metabolism is light because it plays a vital role in synchronizing the circadian clock. Ancient humans started their day at sunrise and ended it at sunset. In modern society, we spend our waking hours indoors under artificial lights and stay up late.

This results in erratic eating habits that wreck our health and sleep. Late at night, organs like the brain, stomach, and gut wind down. Our intestines and gut don't move food down the digestive tract. Therefore, if you eat late and go to bed, the food just sits there, and the stomach starts to produce acid, which results in acid reflux.

It is essential to eat early and have plenty of time between your last meal and bedtime. If you are serious about health and longevity, you need a good metabolism.

According to a study published today in the Endocrine Society's Journal of Clinical Endocrinology & Metabolism, a late dinner might result in weight gain and high blood sugar levels.
Source: https://academic.oup.com/jcem/article/105/8/2789/5855227?login=true

Here we offer some suggestions to get you on the right track:

Hack 86: Improve Metabolic Flexibility:

To accomplish this, begin with the following:

- **Exercise and resistance training.** High-intensity workouts and lifting weights will help your body select the right fuel for the job.
- **Cut down on carbs**. Eliminate refined grains and sugar. Eat high-quality complex carbs. Add more fiber-rich food. Consume good fats and proteins.
- **Practice regular intermittent fasting.** This is discussed in detail in the next chapter.
- **Practice fasted activity**. This means exercising on an empty stomach.

Hack 87: Ensure You Have a High BMR:

Begin by finding what your BMR is. Use one of the many calculators on the Internet, making sure that they factor in activity level for the most accurate reading. This will provide a baseline if you have specific goals, like weight loss.

- Eat a relatively protein-rich diet. Proteins are hard for the body to break down; therefore, it burns more calories in the process.
- Eat high-quality carbs.
- Add spice to your food. Capsaicin, a compound found in spices like jalapeño and cayenne, stimulate your body to release more adrenaline, speeding up your metabolism.
- Add resistance training to your daily routine.
- Get enough sleep.
- Drink green tea regularly.
- Drink plenty of water – ½ liter of water can increase your BMR by 15-20% for an hour.

"Periodic fasting can help clear up the mind and strengthen the body and the spirit."
-Ezra Taft Benson

30

FASTING AND AUTOPHAGY

"Fasting is the first principle of medicine." – Rumi

Our ancestors frequently went with little or no food, albeit not by choice. As unpleasant as that seems to us, fasting is beneficial in many ways. As mentioned in the previous chapter, our bodies have lost metabolic flexibility by eating as much as we like around the clock. We cannot burn fat unless we engage in rigorous exercise and diet regimens. Worse still, we miss out on the beneficial effects of fasting.

Understanding Fasting:

Fasting means willingly abstaining from eating. It has been observed in religions like Christianity, Islam, Judaism, Buddhism, and Hinduism as a spiritual practice for centuries. In medicine, it is often required before surgery or for diagnostic reasons. These types of fasting serve specific purposes, but here we will look at how fasting can improve our health. Two terms are making a splash lately, "intermittent fasting" and "time-restricted feeding." These are essentially the same thing, the only difference being that time-restricted feeding sounds less challenging than fasting.

Intermittent fasting involves consuming zero calories for long periods every day. It ensures that the body goes into a fat-burning state regularly, which is impossible with a regular meal schedule of breakfast, lunch, and dinner. If you're always giving the body calories, it will not start burning stored fat as fuel. So, how long must you fast for that to happen? There are slight variations in the suggested timeframe, but, in general, the 16/8 rule applies – you fast for 14-16 hours each day, restricting your eating window to 8-10 hours.

It's important to understand that intermittent fasting is different from traditional calorie restriction. When a person restricts their calorie intake, they consume fewer calories and typically eat less. Fasting may or may not result in calorie restriction, depending on how much food a person consumes during feeding periods.

The Benefits of Intermittent Fasting:

When you don't eat for a while, your body initiates important processes and changes. Blood levels of insulin drop significantly, facilitating fat burning. Human growth hormone levels may increase as much as five-fold, increasing fat burning and muscle gain, among other benefits.

The body also initiates repair processes, like removing waste material from cells. There are beneficial changes in genes and molecules related to longevity and protection against disease.

The eating and fasting cycles also align with the body's innate circadian system. This may increase metabolic rate, reduce the risk of diabetes, cancer, Alzheimer's, and heart disease, lower oxidative stress, and inflammation, which are key drivers for many diseases.

Autophagy:

The 2016 Nobel Prize in Medicine was awarded to Yoshinori Ohsumi for his discoveries of autophagy mechanisms. The term comes from the Greek *auto* (self) and *phagein* (to eat) and literally means to eat oneself. Essentially, this is how the body gets rid of what is old and deteriorated.

Well-known cardiologist Dr. Luiza Petre describes it as an "evolutionary self-preservation mechanism through which the body can remove the dysfunctional cells and recycle parts of them toward cellular repair and cleaning." Compared to decluttering and organizing your closet, autophagy increases lifespan because it…

- Boosts immunity and fights diseases like cancer, Parkinson's, Alzheimer's, osteoporosis, diabetes, heart disease, muscle loss, etc.
- Improves cellular health and has anti-aging benefits.
- Increases metabolic rate.
- Helps regulate inflammation.
- Helps fight diseases like mycobacterium tuberculosis or viruses, such as HIV.

It's important to note that most of the research on fasting and autophagy has been done on animals, so there's no incontrovertible scientific proof that it works in humans. However, you can give it a try.

How to Trigger Autophagy:

Nutrient deprivation is the key activator, meaning zero calorie intake. What turns autophagy off? Eating, and it doesn't take much. Even a small amount of amino acid (leucine) could stop it. While there are drugs that increase autophagy, it is always preferable to do this naturally. The Ketogenic Diet, exercise, and fasting trigger it, as well as the following foods:

- **Cacao.** Known to induce autophagy in liver cells, it protects the body from cardiovascular diseases. Remember to consume dark chocolate only.
- **Organic olive oil.** Olive oil has many health benefits, including inducing autophagy in the brain and reducing the risk of Alzheimer's disease.
- **Curcumin.** Curcumin is the main active ingredient in turmeric, which is used for skin issues and as an antiseptic. Consuming curcumin increases autophagy in pancreatic cells and also works on Lyme disease.
- **Green tea.** A powerful cup, green tea induces autophagy in every organ of the body!
- **Organic coffee.** Heart and liver show an increase in autophagy after consuming coffee. That said, do not increase your coffee consumption as that might have side effects.

Many studies are being conducted on autophagy, and the results are pending. As such, we must include a word of warning. Autophagy promotes cellular survival, which can be a double edged sword, as both the good and bad cells can get stronger. It may spin-off toward cancer proliferation if other physiological processes are not working properly. Consult your doctor before trying autophagy or rigorous fasting.

The hacks below will improve your eating habits and combine them with a less rigorous fasting practice:

Hack 88: 16:8 Fasting:

This approach extends the feeding window to 8 hours, giving enough time to the body to rest and regenerate during sleep without having to break down food from late-night eating. For example, if you eat dinner at 6 PM, no more food until 10 AM.

Hack 89: Say No to Snacking:

Take your three meals a day but stop munching on snacks in-between.

Hack 90: Combine Keto and Intermittent Fasting:

Again, consult with your doctor before trying this hack, but you may be able to jumpstart weight loss by combining a Keto diet with comfortable intermittent fasting like 12:12. Essentially, this means that you limit eating to a specific window and eat a Ketogenic or Paleo diet within that timeframe.

31

HYDRATION

"Water is the world's first and foremost medicine." – Slovakian proverb

Who hasn't heard the advice about drinking more water? While fasting seems to be beneficial to health, dehydration is unquestionably detrimental. Sufficient hydration is crucial because the human body is comprised mostly of water.

The average percentages vary by gender, age, and weight, but they are staggeringly high. At birth, the body is composed of 75-78% water. In the average adult, it is 57-60%. So, where is all this water? Plasma, the liquid portion of blood, is composed of 90% water. The brain and heart store 73% water, the lungs 83%, the skin 64%, the muscles and kidneys 79%, and the bones 31%.

It's no wonder that, without sufficient water, body functions begin to shut down. The effects of dehydration are: severe anxiety and confusion; inability to stand, walk, or stay awake; faintness not relieved by lying down; rapid breathing; a weak, rapid pulse; loss of consciousness; kidney failure; seizures; swelling in the brain.

The Benefits of Hydration:

Saying that sufficient hydration has benefits is somewhat of a misnomer in the sense that water is fundamental to health. Let's look at some functions more closely.

- **Oral health and digestion:** Water is the main component of saliva, which is essential for breaking down solid food and keeping your mouth healthy.

- **Body temperature:** Sweating keeps you cool in hot environments, but your body temperature will rise if you don't replenish the lost water. That's because your body loses electrolytes and plasma when it's dehydrated.
- **Takes care of your heart:** Working continuously for a couple of hours will leave you craving for water. Then, imagine the amount of water your heart might be craving working all 24 hours without taking a single break! When you are dehydrated, there's a drop in your blood volume, and your heart will have to put in more effort to ensure oxygen distribution throughout your body. Too much pressure on the heart leads to heart-related conditions. If you can prevent all this by drinking enough water, then why not!
- **Physical performance:** Hydration levels affect energy, strength, power, and endurance. You are more susceptible to dehydration if you're participating in endurance training or high-intensity sports.
- **Lubrication:** Water lubricates and cushions the joints, spinal cord, and tissues – this helps you enjoy physical activity and lessens discomfort caused by conditions like arthritis.
- **Detoxification:** Water helps excrete waste through perspiration, urination, and defecation.
- **Weight loss and metabolism:** Drinking more water while dieting and exercising supports weight loss. One study found that drinking 500 milliliters of water boosts the metabolic rate by 30%.
- **Nutrition, oxygenation, circulation:** Water carries nutrients and oxygen to your entire body, also improving circulation.
- **Protection against illness:** Water helps fight conditions like kidney stones, constipation, exercise-induced asthma, urinary tract infections, and hypertension.
- **Cognition and mood:** Not drinking enough water can negatively impact focus, alertness, and short-term memory. It may also result in confusion and anxiety.
- **Skin health:** Adequate water intake will keep your skin hydrated and promote collagen production.

The following hacks will help you establish a routine that has you drinking lots of water:

Hack 91: Calculate and Drink Your Optimum Amount Daily:

You know you are drinking enough water if you rarely feel thirsty and your urine is pale yellow, clear, or cloudy. Drink lots before and after exercise. And, of course, whenever you're thirsty.

Doctors advise that women drink at least 11 cups per day and men a minimum of 16. Keeping in mind that in high temperatures and with physical activity, you should increase your intake, this simple formula will help you find a baseline for your body.

> *Water (in liters) to drink a day = Your Weight (in Kg) multiplied by 0.033.*

Hack 92: Don't Wait Until You Feel Thirsty:

Feeling thirsty is your body's signal that you are **already** dehydrated. Having a personal water bottle, which you take everywhere, will help you stay hydrated and keep track of your intake. Put your bottle on your nightstand to conveniently sip on, should you wake up at night.

Hack 93: Use an App:

If you are busy and tend to forget, install an app to remind you to drink water throughout the day. Set the goal, and the app will help you achieve it.

Hack 94: Make Better Hydration Choices:

If you love sipping on something throughout the day, replace coffee and sugary drinks with unsweetened coconut water, herb-infused water, or functional teas that have so many other health benefits, in addition to hydration.

"Stay active no matter how busy your life is. A quick workout is better than no workout."

# 32

ACTIVE LIFESTYLE

"Walking is man's best medicine." – Hippocrates

Did you know that taking less than 5,000 steps a day is considered sedentary? It seems like a lot, doesn't it? Unfortunately, many of us are glued to our seats all day, especially since working from home became the new normal. Making a concerted effort to stay physically active is more of a priority than ever. An active lifestyle typically includes an exercise regimen, but it is not limited to it. Having an active lifestyle means moving your body as much as possible to the level of your ability, whether you are seventeen or seventy years old.

The Benefits of Movement:

As we can see from the following list of benefits, physical activity plays a huge role in health and well-being:

- **Weight management:** The more you move, the more calories you burn. Exercise can prevent excess weight gain or maintain weight loss.
- **Defense against illness:** Regular exercise helps prevent or manage conditions like stroke, metabolic syndrome, hypertension, type 2 diabetes, depression, anxiety, cancer, and arthritis.
- **Strong bones, muscles, and joints:** Regular exercise lowers the risk of osteoporosis and other bone/joint-related diseases. By strengthening the musculoskeletal structure, it can help prevent falls in the elderly.

- **Mood and cognition:** Movement releases endorphins, which put you in a good mood. It also improves cognitive functions. According to Thomas Mann, *"Thoughts come clearly while one walks."*
- **Confidence and appearance:** Being fit boosts your self-esteem and improves your looks.
- **Energy and sex:** Regular physical activity improves energy levels in everyone. It may enhance sexual arousal in women, while men are less likely to have problems with erectile dysfunction.
- **Fun, social engagement:** Physical activity is a chance to unwind, enjoy the outdoors, and do activities with family or friends, like playing sports.
- **Better sleep:** Exercise helps you fall asleep and stay asleep but don't do it too close to bedtime, or you may be too energized.

What Type of Exercise and How Much?

Naturally, the type and duration of exercise appropriate for each person depend on their age and health condition. For most healthy adults, the US Department of Health and Human Services recommends:

- At least 150 minutes of moderate aerobic activity or 75 minutes of vigorous aerobic activity or a combination of the two spread throughout the week. Examples include running, walking, or swimming. To lose weight, you may need to ramp up moderate aerobic activity to 300 minutes or more per week.
- Strength training (weight lifting) for all major muscle groups at least twice a week.

The following hacks will help you develop an active lifestyle that is best suited to your lifestyle and needs:

Hack 95: Consult Your Doctor and Find A Coach:

If you have medical conditions, speak to your doctor before you start a new regimen. Exercise, especially when vigorous, can strain the heart, lungs, and joints. Make sure that you do not exacerbate any pre-existing conditions or put yourself at risk. After consulting your doctor, it would be advisable to have a qualified fitness coach design the appropriate routine for your physical condition.

Hack 96: Home Workouts:

If you are unable to go outside or do not want to, you can do these exercises indoors:

- Stretching improves flexibility and range of motion. It also improves blood circulation. Walk or jog around your garden or terrace.
- Jumping rope is of the best exercises you can do at home.
- Squats and lunges keep you fit and tone your muscles. When you first start, ask someone to monitor you; you need to do them correctly to get maximum benefits.
- Jumping jacks are easy to do even in small spaces.

Start any new routine slowly and increase the duration gradually. It may be more effective to break it down into shorter intervals. The Harvard School of Public Health indicates that three 10-minute sessions were as good as one longer session. Remember always to warm up to avoid injury.

Hack 97: Tips to Stay Active:

If you despise working out, and nothing can convince you to hit the gym, these suggestions will help you remain active:

- **Walk everywhere:** If your destination is very far away, take public transport part of the way or park at a distance. Listening to music while walking improves mood. Impact forces on the feet can total several hundred tons, so invest in quality footwear. If you can't wear sneakers all day, bring a change of shoes with you.
- **Take the stairs:** Stair climbing is considered the ultimate calorie burner. It's also great cardio.

- **Cook and clean:** Sweeping and mopping are great workouts. A 150-pound person can burn between 85-102 calories per half-hour by cleaning. They can burn up to 78 calories in 30 minutes of cooking! As a bonus, home-cooked food is always healthier because you control the ingredients.
- **Dance:** Dancing burns around 200 calories every half-hour.
- **Mind and body**: If you prefer or require low-impact exercise, consider Yoga, Pilates, and Tai Chi. You will move your body and practice mindfulness at the same time.

Hack 98: Use Apps:

To reach your goals, use a fitness app or wearable to track how many steps you have taken each day. Set reminders so you can get up from your desk and move around at regular intervals. Studies show that moving every 30 minutes can minimize the negative effects of a sedentary lifestyle.

33

SLEEP

"Sleep is the golden chain that ties health and our bodies together."
- Thomas Dekker

When a living being is completely at rest, its body has the opportunity to direct energy to healing functions. While in the Rapid Eye Movement (REM) phase, the brain is very active with dreams, memory consolidation, learning, and problem-solving; the deep sleep state is the most restorative.

Sleep allows the body to repair itself, improve immunity and heart health, reduce stress and inflammation, balance hormones, and reduce the risk of cancer. It increases energy, strength, brain-body coordination, flexibility, and flight-fight responses. It allows for the regeneration of cells and brain detoxification from proteins associated with Alzheimer's. It also allows for the formation of new neuropathways to process information and improve memory, learning, attention, creativity, and decision-making.

Dreaming helps us sort experiences and memories to store what is important. According to Harvard Psychiatry Professor Robert Stickgold, *"When we dream, we get the pieces. When we wake, we can know the whole."*

Sleep Deprivation:

According to The National Sleep Foundation, an adult needs 7-9 hours of sleep every night. Workaholics profess that sleep is a waste of time, jesting, "I'll sleep when I'm dead." Well, it's not a laughing matter because you **can die** from extreme sleep deprivation. Beyond the obvious risk of accidents, research shows that you are two to three times more likely to have a heart attack if you sleep less than five hours per night. In women, the risk is even greater. Even if sleep deprivation does not kill you, its effects are detrimental, as illustrated by the following story:

> *In 1963, 17-year-old Randy Gardner entered a science fair with the goal of staying awake for eleven days. He and two friends broke the world record, while researchers monitored closely. Two days into the contest, Randy showed symptoms of ataxia (lack of voluntary coordination of muscle movements that can include gait abnormality, speech changes, and abnormalities in eye movements). By day three, he had become moody and uncoordinated; he started hallucinating by day five. His condition worsened as days passed. He had serious trouble concentrating and experienced short-term memory loss. His speech became slurred, and his attention span was very short. His mental abilities diminished severely. After learning about these effects, Guinness stopped listing records for sleep deprivation to put a stop to further attempts.*

As we can see from the following list, long-term sleep deprivation adversely impacts both health and well-being:

- **Physical:** The effects include lowered immunity, infections, respiratory diseases; weight gain and obesity; higher risk of cardiovascular disease and stroke; hormonal imbalances with increased stress hormones and reduced fertility; hypertension; sleep apnea.
- **Emotional:** Sleep deprivation affects the amygdala, which deals with emotion, resulting in difficulty controlling responses and coping with change. It can lead to depression, anxiety, and psychosis, with an increased risk of suicide and risk-taking behaviors.
- **Mental:** Lack of sleep negatively impacts the brain's prefrontal cortex, which handles reasoning, decision-making, problem-solving, etc.

Insomnia:

Sleeplessness is a common problem that affects people's quality of life and ability to thrive. They have trouble falling asleep or staying asleep. When the problem is chronic, a medical diagnosis is required that involves a physical examination and blood tests to look for any underlying conditions. Insomnia disorder can be a symptom of:

- **Circadian rhythm:** Circadian rhythm sleep disorders share the common feature of a disruption in the timing of sleep. Typically, they are related to work and lifestyle (e.g., jet lag, shift work, high altitudes).
- **Hormones:** Whether caused by menopause, pregnancy, or adrenal fatigue, hormonal shifts can cause insomnia, worsening – in turn – the hormone imbalance.
- **Medical conditions:** Examples include chronic pain, cancer, diabetes, heart disease, asthma, gastroesophageal reflux disease (GERD), overactive thyroid, Parkinson's, Alzheimer's, parasites, etc.
- **Medications:** Many prescription medications interfere with sleep (e.g., antidepressants, asthma, blood pressure medications). Over-the-counter medications (e.g., pain, allergy, flu, and weight loss) contain stimulants that can also disrupt sleep.
- **Sleep-related disorders:** Sleep apnea leads to difficulty in breathing throughout the night, interrupting sleep. Restless legs syndrome causes unpleasant sensations in the legs, preventing you from sleeping.
- **Mental health:** Insomnia often occurs in tandem with PTSD, depression, bipolar disorder, psychotic disorders, and anxiety disorders.
- **Stress:** An overactive mind, which prevents you from relaxing enough to sleep, can result from concerns over family and finance or from stressful life events like death and divorce.
- **Poor sleep habits:** Irregular bedtime schedules, naps, an uncomfortable sleep environment, and using your bed for work or entertainment (e.g., computers, TVs, video games, smartphones) can disrupt sleep cycles.
- **Caffeine, nicotine, and alcohol:** Smoking and drinking caffeinated beverages in the late afternoon or evening can keep you from falling asleep. Alcohol may help you fall asleep but prevents deep sleep, causing awakening in the middle of the night.

If you are having trouble sleeping, whether chronically or occasionally, the following hacks will help you get a full night of restorative sleep:

Hack 99: Tips for a Good Night's Sleep:

Simple, easy, everyday suggestions to maximize the quality of your sleep:

- Avoid eating 2–3 hours before bedtime.
- Avoid caffeine and alcohol, especially close to bedtime.
- Sleep in a dark, quiet, and cool room.
- Invest in a quality mattress and pillows.
- Remove all electronic devices from the bedroom.
- A shower or bath before bed relaxes your body and makes you feel like you have washed the day away.
- Get regular exercise during the day.
- Avoid tobacco.
- If your partner's snoring prevents you from sleeping, address their problem as well.
- If your mind is racing about the things you have to do the next day, making a schedule might put your mind at ease.

Hack 100: Dealing with Insomnia:

If you have chronic insomnia, seek professional advice. If it's an occasional problem, in addition to the above tips, the following may help:

- After trying to fall asleep for 20 minutes, get up and read, then try again later. There are many prescription and over-the-counter sleep aids, but first, try a functional tea like chamomile or lavender to help you unwind. If you need something to put you to sleep, try a valerian root tea.
- Switch to a whole-food, plant-based diet rich in fruit, vegetables, legumes, nuts, and whole grains.
- Try sleep restriction therapy, which reduces the time spent in bed to match your sleep hours closely. It is often used with stimulus control therapy, which strengthens the association between bed and sleep by using the bed only for sleep and sex.
- Breathing and muscle relaxation techniques can improve sleep quality. Also, create a bedtime ritual. This may involve showering, drinking a functional tea, preparing your space for sleep, meditating, etc.

34

MEDITATION

*Meditation will not carry you to another world, but it will reveal the
most profound and awesome dimensions of the world in which you already live.
Calmly contemplating these dimensions and bringing them
into the service of compassion and kindness is the
right way to make rapid gains
in meditation as well as in life."
– Zen Master Hsing Yun*

The word "meditation" is everywhere these days, not only because people are looking to relieve stress but also "live consciously." By increasing self-awareness, meditation helps achieve that goal. What is meditation exactly? A single, definitive explanation is elusive because meditation means many things and has many objectives. There also are various types, techniques, and approaches, both ancient and contemporary. Yet, the verb "to meditate" means to think deeply or focus one's mind for some time, either for relaxation or religious or spiritual purposes. The synonyms "contemplation, musing, pondering, reflection, and prayer" help unfold the meaning further.

Meditation trains attention and awareness. It brings mental clarity and emotional calmness by concentrating on an object, thought, sound, or activity. It also means going inward, connecting with one's higher mind, thereby enabling inspiration, problem-solving, deeper understanding, even deep transcendental states, like *Samadhi*, where the individual becomes absorbed in higher states of consciousness for some time.

As Ma Jaya Sati Bhagavati said, "*Quiet the mind, and the soul will speak*."

Benefits of Meditation:

Managing our thoughts and emotional reactions has many benefits. The following findings are based on science and supported by many studies:

- **Stress:** Meditation can reduce stress and symptoms of stress-triggered conditions like PTSD, IBS, and fibromyalgia.
- **Anxiety:** Meditation reduces social anxiety, phobias, and obsessive-compulsive behaviors.
- **Depression:** Ongoing practice alleviates depression and creates a more positive long-term outlook.
- **Attention span:** Some types of meditation improve the ability to redirect and maintain attention.
- **Self-awareness:** Meditation helps you "know yourself," which is the starting point for positive life changes.
- **Memory:** The improved focus gained through meditation increases memory and mental clarity, helping fight age-related memory loss and dementia.
- **Kindness:** Metta, or loving-kindness meditation, increases empathy and compassionate behavior.
- **Addiction:** Meditation develops mental discipline and willpower that help resist triggers and impulses, thereby controlling unwanted habits and addictions.
- **Sleep:** Some forms help you relax and control 'runaway' thoughts, shortening the time it takes to fall asleep and increasing sleep quality.
- **Pain:** Meditation can diminish the perception of pain in the brain. When used in conjunction with medical care, it can help manage chronic pain.
- **Hypertension:** Blood pressure decreases not only during meditation but also over time in individuals who meditate regularly.

Types of Meditation:

There are many types of meditation, each with a specific approach and goal.

- **Mindfulness meditation:** The most popular form in the West originates from Buddhism; Vipassana involves observing your thoughts and emotions without judging or dwelling in them.
- **Spiritual meditation:** Used in eastern religions, like Hinduism, Daoism, and Christianity, it aims at spiritual growth.
- **Focused meditation:** Ideal for anyone requiring additional focus, for the practice involves concentration using any of the five senses. Try counting mala beads, listening to a gong, or staring at a candle flame.
- **Movement meditation:** Gentle forms of movement like walking, gardening, and qigong are suited for people who find peace in action and prefer to let their minds wander.
- **Mantra meditation:** Prominent in Hindu and Buddhist traditions, a repetitive sound like "Om" is used to clear the mind and experience deeper levels of awareness.
- **Transcendental meditation:** This practice also uses mantras or a series of words. It works well for those who like structure.
- **Progressive relaxation:** Also known as "body-scan meditation," this practice reduces tension in the body and promotes relaxation, for example, before bedtime.
- **Loving-kindness meditation:** Used to strengthen compassion, kindness, and acceptance toward oneself and others.
- **Visualization meditation:** The technique creates relaxation, peace, and calmness by visualizing positive images. It also increases focus and motivation by imagining achieving specific goals.
- **The Silva Method:** Developed by Jose Silva in 1960, it aims to enhance a person's skills and develop higher brain functions and psychic abilities such as clairvoyance and extrasensory perception.
- **Binaural beats:** Brain entrainment using sound; it produces specific brainwave states, like Delta (1-4Hz), Theta (4-8Hz), Alpha (8-14Hz), Beta (14-30Hz), Gamma (30-100Hz), each with its own benefits, like relaxation, pain relief, creativity, accelerated learning, memory, and transcendental states.
- **Guided meditation:** Meditation with the guidance of an experienced practitioner who takes you through relaxation techniques and visualizations with specific goals.

The benefits of adopting a regular practice are substantial. If you have never explored meditation or think that it's not for you, you may find the following helpful:

Hack 101: Problems and Solutions:

There are many reasons why meditation does not come easily to everyone. Here, we address the most common obstacles.
"I can't clear my mind." If you have a "monkey mind," try mindfulness meditation, which makes you fully aware of your thoughts in the present moment. **"I get restless."** If you find it impossible to sit still, try a moving meditation. **"I can't do the lotus posture."** Then don't! Sit on a chair or lie down. What's important is that you are comfortable enough to unwind.
"I don't have enough time." If you cannot spare time during the day, then do it before you fall asleep or as soon as you wake up in the morning.
"I fall asleep." Stretch beforehand and meditate sitting up. Do it during a time of day when you are most alert. **"I can't stick with it."** Yes, but you can start again today. Don't just quit; keep trying. **"I won't be good at it."** Many people doubt themselves and give up. Practice makes perfect.

Hack 102: Find the Best Practice for You:

Start by identifying your goals. Are you looking for spiritual growth, improved concentration, or relaxation? Keep in mind that you can practice several forms for different reasons.

Hack 103: Create a Sanctuary:

If you design a beautiful, quiet, private, and comfortable space, not only will you be eager to retreat there but also get into the mood more quickly. A comfortable chair or daybed, plush pillows, incense, crystals, music, art, even your personal altar will help.

Hack 104: Apps, Guided Meditations, Binaural Beats:

These work well for beginners, especially if you have difficulty relaxing or clearing your mind.

35

BREATHWORK

"When the breath is unsteady, all is unsteady; when the breath is still, all is still. Control the breath carefully." – Goraksha Satakam

Intrinsically tied to some meditation forms, breathwork originates in ancient spiritual practices like yoga, Tai Chi, Buddhism, and other mystical traditions. Breathing may be an involuntary function but getting the full benefit takes conscious effort. As babies, we breathe from the belly but gradually shift out of that "belly breathing" to a more shallow and less healthful "chest breathing." Deep breathing is done by contracting the diaphragm, the horizontal muscle between the thorax and abdomen. When air enters the lungs, it is the belly that expands, not the chest – this allows for maximum intake of oxygen and expulsion of carbon dioxide in every breath. The practice of consciously changing one's breathing patterns is called breathwork, which has many types, each with its benefits and purposes.

The Benefits of Breathwork:

Surprising as it may seem, breathing impacts not only the body but also the emotions, mind, and spirit. Let's examine each area more closely.

- **Body:** Breathwork expert Dan Brule considers the practice as essential preventive medicine for the 21st century. Breathwork boosts lung volume and prevents the loss of lung capacity that comes with age. It improves posture and spinal health, weakened due to sedentary lifestyles. During stressful moments, cortisol and adrenaline quicken the pulse and raise blood pressure, putting the body-mind in a state of hypervigilance.

- The fight-or-flight response is essential if you are in physical danger but harmful on a daily basis. Deep breathing can reverse this response and relax the body, often immediately. It activates the parasympathetic nervous system, lowering heart rate and blood pressure. When done consistently, it also improves immune function, alkalizing the blood and decreasing inflammation. It also gives you more energy and vitality.
- **Emotions and mind:** Deep breathing helps calm a turbulent mind. It can help you access buried emotions, grudges, and traumas so that you can release yourself from their grip. Breathwork is effective in treating depression, anxiety, and PTSD. It also increases joy, creativity, mental clarity, and focus.

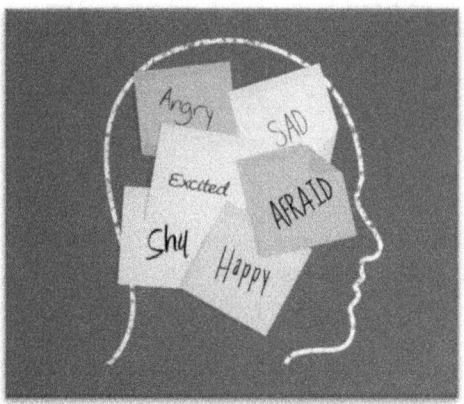

- **Spirit:** As a meditative practice, observing or controlling the breath puts you in a state of mindfulness by quieting the mind and keeping you in the present moment. Breathwork has been used in spiritual traditions for ages because it helps you connect with your spirit. It can lead to spiritual insights and awakenings, as well as mystical experiences.

Types of Breathwork:

Shamanic, Transformational, Radiance, Clarity, Integrative, Neurodynamic, Ecstatic, Ananda – there are numerous breathwork techniques, but the most popular are:

- **Pranayama:** The world's best-known practice comes from yoga. Learning to control *prana*, which means breath or life force, is a crucial aspect of this tradition. When yoga is used as exercise, the breath is synchronized with the movement between *asanas* (postures).

As a spiritual practice, Pranayama originates in the *Bhagavad Gita*, where it is described as a trance induced by stopping all breathing. It is considered an integral step on the path to enlightenment.
- **Holotropic Breathwork:** Created by psychiatrists Christina and Stanislav Grof, this therapeutic technique uses breathing patterns to create an altered state of consciousness, where the individual can address physical, emotional, and spiritual pain. It treats depression, PTSD, chronic pain, and avoidance behaviors.
- **Wim Hof Method:** Extreme athlete Wim Hof developed his own technique to keep his body in optimal condition in extreme weather conditions. Many physical and mental health benefits include enhancing sports performance, cold tolerance, willpower, metabolism, and improving Parkinson's, arthritis, asthma, COPD, and several autoimmune disorders.
- **Rebirthing Breathwork:** Developed by Leonard Orr in the 1960s, it provides a therapeutic effect by releasing unprocessed or repressed emotions. Often too difficult or painful to deal with at the time of the traumatic event, they impact mental health and the physical body.

Speak to your doctor before beginning any breathwork therapy, especially if you have a medical condition that may be affected by the practice. This includes if you are pregnant or breastfeeding.

Hack 105: Simple Breathing Techniques:

The following suggestions can be done by anyone at any moment:

- **Lengthen your exhale for stress release**: When you feel agitated, stop what you are doing, and take a deep breath. However, taking too many deep breaths too quickly can cause you to hyperventilate. Before you take a deep breath, push all the air out of your lungs, and then let them do their work.
- **Learn breath focus for mindfulness:** To center yourself, simply observe your breath without trying to control it. Focus your attention on the air passing to your lungs, feeling the expansion in your chest and belly.
- **Relearn belly breathing for better health:** Diaphragmatic breathing reduces the work your body needs to do and maximizes oxygenation. For this type of breathing to become automatic, you'll need to practice it daily.

"The secret to living well and longer is: eat half. walk double, laugh triple and love without measure."
- Tibetan Proverb

36

LONGEVITY AND ANTI-AGEING

"Getting older is inevitable, aging... is optional."
— *Dr. Christiane Northrup*

We close this section with a chapter meant to inspire and empower you. So far, we have presented lifestyles and modalities that can help you achieve optimum health and wellness. Can you do more? Can you thrive into ripe old age, and what age is that exactly? The Bible says that Methuselah lived to be 969 years old. However, the greatest fully-authenticated age is 122 years 164 days – Jeanne Louise Calment.

We have all met people who are twenty but look forty and vice versa. Is it genetics or lifestyle? Wrinkles, weight gain, poor memory, and aches indicate 'abnormal' aging even later in life, according to biohacker Dave Asprey, who advocates taking control of our biology by changing our inner and outer environment.

Endocrinologist and spiritual teacher Deepak Chopra corroborates that a healthy lifestyle can "add up to 30 to 50 years to your life, in both quality and quantity. These things override the genes."

World-renewed aging expert David A. Sinclair believes that lifespan is 80% lifestyle and 20% genetics. Aging can definitely be delayed with genetic, dietary, and pharmacologic approaches. The body has an excellent repair system that we can optimize through lifestyle and outlook.

Harvard psychologist Ellen Langer tested the theory that strength, posture, memory, hearing, and vision might be improved using psychological intervention alone.

In her experiment, eight men in their seventies were asked to live as though they were twenty years younger in a controlled setting that recreated the world at that time – news, clothing, music, etc.

After one week, there was a significant improvement in their physical strength, dexterity, gait, posture, perception, memory, cognition, taste, sensitivity, hearing, and vision!

How one thinks is fundamental to how well the body repairs itself, as proven by spontaneous remissions like the well-documented cases in Deepak Chopra's groundbreaking book *Quantum Healing*. All the above-said things suggest that mind-body synergy can contribute to longevity, possibly even youthing.

Youthing:

The idea of slowing, stopping, or reversing aging has been around for centuries. In modern times, homeopathic physician Gabriel Cousens coined the term "youthing" after discovering that it "happens when more new cells are produced than that are dying." He advocates juice, fasting, and other methods like a restricted calorie diet. Another youthing pioneer, Viktoras Kulvinskas, is known as the father of the raw food movement. He also promotes live enzymes as sources of health and youth.

Chiropractor, personal trainer, and author George Cromack takes a comprehensive approach, "With multi-pronged strategies, you can get a better full-bodied and more complete result." David Sinclair makes no recommendations to others except "Eat fewer calories," "Don't sweat the small stuff," and "Exercise." However, he has been testing his theories on himself. He has been following the regimen we relay here – not as a suggestion – only to show that most components are aligned with what we have discussed in this book.

- He limits sugar, bread, and pasta, doesn't eat desserts, and avoids meat.
- He skips one meal a day.
- He stays active, jogs, lifts weights, uses the sauna, and then dunks in an ice-cold pool.
- He maintains a BMI of 23-25.
- He doesn't smoke.
- He avoids microwaved plastic, excessive UV exposure, X-rays, and CT scans.
- He tries to keep environmental temperatures on the cool side.
- He takes vitamin D, vitamin K2, and aspirin.
- He takes nicotinamide mononucleotide, resveratrol, and metformin daily.
- He monitors biomarkers with frequent blood tests and tries to adjust them with food and exercise.

"It's impossible to say if my regimen is working, but it doesn't seem to be hurting," Sinclair acknowledges, claiming he feels the same at 50 as he did at 30. Feeling young and vital is what matters; age is just a number.

Some think of longevity in terms of years only, but we mean many years lived thriving!

Hack 106: Mind-Body Synergy:

The following suggestions summarize what we have discussed in this section while adding a few elements.

Fasting: Research shows that a 12% caloric restriction decreased the risk of many fatal diseases. Intermittent fasting has also proven to be very helpful.

Organics and supplements: Even if you avoid processed foods, industrialized food is nutritionally depleted and contains harmful chemicals like pesticides. Eat organic as often as possible, especially when it comes to functional herbs and supplements because their therapeutic benefits will be potent and complete. Take supplements as needed, like Vitamin D in winter if you live in a cold climate where sunlight is unavailable daily.

Oxygenation: Tel Aviv University and Shamir Medical Centre found that Hyperbaric Oxygen Therapy reversed critical indicators of aging. You may not have access to an oxygen chamber like Michael Jackson but can maximize oxygenation with breathwork. Clean air will do wonders for your mind and body – get as much as you can.

Mind over matter: Your body is always listening to your words and thoughts. If you believe that you will deteriorate with age, it will create that reality. Using visualizations, guided meditations, and affirmations, you can communicate anti-aging instructions to your body.

Hack 107: Safe Biohacking:

Although some forms of biohacking are extreme and risky, the term simply means making changes to optimize the way the body functions. There are two ways to try it safely and effectively:

- For specific health concerns, biohacking can mean treating the problem, not only the symptoms. Instead of relying only on allopathic medicine to manage the issue, explore alternative healing modalities (e.g., Ayurveda, traditional Chinese medicine, naturopathy) to address the underlying condition.
- If you are healthy, you can test your body's responses to specific changes, thereby finding natural ways to improve the way you feel. Biohacks include strategies like trying an elimination or raw food diet.

"In the end, we only regret the chances we didn't take."

LIVE YOUR HIGHEST JOY
Tomorrow is uncertain. So, live your present to the fullest!

"If you could see the potential within you, it would amaze you to see all that you are capable of being."
-Catherine Pulsifer

37

HAPPINESS AND FULFILLMENT

> *"To get the full value of joy, you must have someone to divide it with."*
> *— Mark Twain*

The feeling of happiness and fulfillment is the reward and natural outcome of thriving. Thriving is defined as "flourishing, prospering, succeeding, increasing," in the dictionary; in our context, the definition includes "feeling happy and fulfilled."

We often misunderstand happiness as the result of things we strive for externally, not as a state of being. As such, many pursue it solely through success, pleasure, and gratification, all of which are short-lived. Others live with the hope that happiness will come their way one day. Typically, it never does. Neither the pursuit of external conditions nor idle hope yields lasting results. What is possible is cultivating happiness!

How? By taking actions, which contribute to happiness in the form of fulfillment, and making some shifts in mindset. Happiness and fulfillment are linked; fulfillment gives rise to joy. Research shows that happy people are better at sustaining relationships, being healthy, and performing well at work. So, fulfillment creates happiness, which creates more fulfillment, and so on. Let's look at how we can create these states of being.

The Keys to Happiness:

Happiness: n. an emotion of joy, gladness, satisfaction, and well-being.

We can add to the definition by borrowing from Sonja Lyubomirsky's book, *The How of Happiness*, which describes it as an experience of joy combined with a sense that one's life is meaningful and worthwhile besides being good.

Most of us need no explanation for the word "happiness" because it is something we feel. And when we don't feel it, we yearn for it. I believe that all living things are hardwired for happiness. So how do we achieve this most desirable state?

- **Value the little things**: Our culture is obsessed with material wealth and a limited definition of success, like that coveted promotion. In an opinion piece in *Time*, Eric Barker noted that focusing on the little things, like beautiful flowers and smiling at passersby, leads to an increased sense of happiness in less than a week.
- **Savor every moment**: Eric Barker also makes a case for enjoying the moment instead of rushing through it. For instance, avoid multitasking, such as watching TV while eating your dinner. Slow down, observe, and enjoy what we consider mundane things, like a refreshing shower after a long day. Be mindful and pay attention to details. It is said that people aware of their surroundings have more robust immune systems and are less hostile.
- **Count your blessings so they can multiply:** The well-known Law of Attraction, which essentially means "like attracts like," asserts that the more you focus on certain situations or feelings (negative or positive), life will keep bringing you more of the same. Positive psychology researchers like Michael McCullough, Emmons, and Lyubomirsky have argued that people who count their blessings and keep gratitude journals feel more optimism and satisfaction in their lives than others.
- **Give thanks for the miracle of your life:** The next time you're feeling low, think of how lucky you are to be able to breathe, see, walk, and speak.
- **Give thanks to and for others:** When your friend does something for you, write a little thank-you-note. At the same time, be thankful that you have a friend who cares so much for you. Small actions and thoughts will boost your happiness and cultivate a grateful disposition.
- **Meaningful relationships:** Surrounding yourself with people that inspire you will do wonders for your mental health. Healthy friendships foster happiness and growth; avoid individuals that drain you.
- **Self-love:** How can anyone be happy if they have self-contempt or are abusing themselves in some way? Say no when someone asks something you cannot do, rather than doing it begrudgingly. Author Daylle Deanna Schwartz says that when you love yourself, you will easily say no because it is an act of kindness to yourself.

We have all heard the saying, "You can't love anyone unless you love yourself" – this certainly does not mean being selfish but showing compassion to yourself and setting boundaries.

- **Reduce stress:** You can't be happy when you're stressed and busy. Take time out to do things you enjoy or relax. Even if life leaves you with little opportunity for leisure, schedule in some "me-time" at least once a day.

  Sign up for a pottery workshop or join a reading club. Take a bubble bath. The key is to keep filling your cup. Self-care is vital for better mental health.

- **Own it all – good, bad, or ugly!** Until you realize that you are responsible for everything in your life, especially how you perceive and react to situations, you cannot achieve happiness. Why? Because you are expecting happiness to come from something "out there."

  To put it plainly, stop blaming other people and situations for your discontent. Take control of your life instead of letting things "just happen to you."

- **Opt for joy; focus on what's good.** Find ways to laugh and have fun rather than allowing yourself to be swept into the mainstream media doom and gloom.

  Play with your dog, watch a comedy show; you can even organize a watch party with friends or family to spread and enhance the cheer. Laughter releases hormones like endorphins, serotonin, and dopamine.

All the above highlights that happiness is a result of perspective, as the following story also illustrates:

> *In a village lived an old man who was the most unfortunate person in the world. He was always in a lousy mood and complained constantly.*
> *People avoided him because his misfortune was contagious. "He creates a feeling of unhappiness in others," they said.*
> *On the day he turned 80, a rumor spread throughout the village, "The old man is happy! He smiles and doesn't complain anymore."*
> *The village folk gathered around the old man and asked the reason for his happiness. "Nothing special," he said.*
> *"For 80 years, I chased happiness, and it was useless.*
> *Now, I've decided to just be and enjoy life.*
> *This is why I am happy now."*

The Keys to Fulfillment:

As the definition indicates, fulfillment is a contributing factor to happiness, but not the same thing as happiness. The distinction is important because while actions do not necessarily create happiness, fulfillment is a feeling that arises from actions, behaviors, and achievement. The keys to fulfillment are:

- **Growth mindset:** Chris Myers, in a piece for *Forbes*, notes that people with a growth mindset are happier than those with a fixed mindset. Those who possess self-awareness and self-compassion learn from setbacks as opposed to merely being upset. They accept, identify, and do their best to overcome their shortcomings without scolding themselves.
- **Self-improvement:** Working on your skills and personality contributes to external success and healthy pride. However, there are a few things to keep in mind: First, define the principles and values that will guide your life, and do your best to apply them. Second, treat others as you wish to be treated. Be generous and kind. For instance, if someone is sick, visit with flowers or help with chores. If someone needs money, do what you can before they ask without making a big show of it.
- **Living life to the fullest:** Make a bucket list and check items off it. Travel, explore new cultures, or do things you think you cannot do. Be open to experiencing nature and doing activities that you usually wouldn't, as this will provide you with a sense of accomplishment.
- **Contributing to society:** Researchers Dunn and Aknin have found that people report greater happiness when they spend money on others than themselves. Likewise, neuroscience shows that our brains light up in areas associated with pleasure and reward when we do good things for others.
  Develop a service mindset. Volunteering at a care home or teaching underprivileged kids can be a rewarding and humbling experience. If motivation is an issue, then pick a cause you deeply care about and contribute to it. In the spirit of making a difference, adopt a stray cat or dog.
  This is an extremely gratifying experience because you will have a little furry friend who will love you unconditionally. Random acts of kindness are the best and the easiest to carry out.

Fulfillment: n. the achievement of something desired, promised, or predicted; satisfaction or happiness as a result of fully developing one's abilities or character.

The following hacks should help you create feelings of joy and fulfillment:

Hack 108: Stay in The Moment:

Most of us tend to live in our past or future, defining ourselves by our memories or expectations. We hold on to past hurts and fear future loss, but the past is gone, and the future is unknown. Learning to live in the present is the only way to stop being haunted by things you have no control over; focus on the 'now moment'. It's the only thing that is real.

Hack 109: Create a Gratitude Journal:

Research shows that developing an attitude of gratefulness transforms individuals and societies for the better. Create a gratitude journal and write in it before going to bed. Make a habit of appreciating at least one small thing every day.

Hack 110: Forgive, Let Go, and Move On:

Let go of grudges because the only person you are hurting is yourself. Other people will not suffer from the toxic feelings that are within you.

Forgiving does not mean you are saying what they did was okay. You do it because you need to feel lighter and focus on things that matter. Also, you can only give to others what you have – if you are filled with anger and resentment, that's what you will project to the world. Make sure you have forgiveness and kindness to share.

Hack 111: Be Brave:

If you are stuck in a relationship, job, or situation that is making you miserable – even if it's just "a thorn in your side" – this prevents you from growing. Be brave enough to go out into the world and seek your happiness.

Hack 112: Do A SWOT Analysis on Yourself:

A term used in business, SWOT is the acronym for strengths, weaknesses, opportunities, and threats. Knowing yourself will make you confident – you will realize you have overcome plenty of obstacles in the past and will continue to do so in the future. You will identify the areas you need to work on, face the challenges and get out of your comfort zone. It will build a growth mindset that is conducive to happiness.

"Worry never robs tomorrow of its sorrow, it only saps today of its joy."
Leo Buscaglia

38

PRACTICE BENEFICIAL WORRYING

"That the birds of worry and care fly over your head, this you cannot change, but that they build nests in your hair, this you can prevent."– Chinese proverb

Worry comes from the fear of the unknown. It is the bane of human existence and a great source of unhappiness. Doubts and anxieties last for a while, then go away. However, when they become constant, there is cause for concern. And when they start to interfere with one's day-to-day activities, the person will be diagnosed with Generalized Anxiety Disorder (GAD). At that stage, the person should consider consulting a mental health professional.

It is crucial to manage negative thoughts and regulate them before they spin out of control. Constant worrying leads to chronic stress, which impairs brain function in multiple ways. It kills brain cells, shrinks its size, and leads to loss of sociability. Not only that, it affects the immune system; it is common knowledge that many physical illnesses are linked to stress.

Furthermore, it impairs cognitive function, thereby interfering in everyday activities. If one wants to thrive, then it's imperative to manage stress and reduce worry.

To deal with worry, anxiety, and stress effectively, we must differentiate between problems that can and cannot be solved. As glaringly obvious as this may sound, instead of fretting pointlessly, deal with those that can be resolved and let go of the others. It never ceases to amaze me how most chronic worries fail to make that basic distinction!

> *A psychology professor, while teaching stress management principles, raised a glass of water. She asked the class, "How heavy is this glass of water?" The students' answers were between 8-12 ounces. The professor then said, "From my perspective, the absolute weight doesn't matter. What matters is time: If I hold the glass for a few minutes, it's fairly light. If I hold it for an hour, it will make my arm ache. Holding it for a day will give my arm a cramp, make it numb, even paralyze it for a while." Intrigued by her analogy, the students listened carefully as she continued, "In each of those scenarios, the weight of the glass doesn't change, but the longer I hold it, the heavier it feels to me. Your worries are very much like this glass of water. Think of them for a while, and nothing happens. Ruminate about them for a day, and it hurts a little. Holding on to it for days will have you feeling numb and paralyzed – incapable of doing anything else until you drop them."*

Here are some suggestions on how to manage worry and stress:

Hack 113: Shift From "What if?" to "How can I?"

Do you tend to assume that something will go wrong, always asking, "What if...?" If yes, you should realize that most scenarios you create in your head are unlikely to happen. In an article for *Psychology Today*, Professor Graham C.L. Davey tackles "what-if-worrying" and points out that one must not waste time picturing the worst scenario; instead, one should focus on how the situation can be managed. The next time you think that something may go wrong, stop yourself and reimagine it going well. You can also weigh a negative outcome in terms of importance. Ask yourself, "Will it matter in five years?" If not, then don't spend more than five minutes on it.

Hack 114: The "I-can-handle-it" Mindset:

Another trick that comes in handy is telling yourself that you'll handle whatever comes your way. This not only gives you a confident disposition but also soothes your mind. Coupled with the "How can I?" hack, this approach will help reduce your stress and become proactive. It's a win-win proposition.

Hack 115: Keep a Worry Diary:

As counter-intuitive as this sounds, it's an excellent approach to sorting out your concerns before they become a tangled mess in your mind. Keeping a worry diary forces you to become conscious of your worries. Note down your thoughts for a week, then separate them into two categories.

On one list, include things you can do nothing about (e.g., "What if Uncle dies?"). On the other, put worries you can address. Ignore the first category. Go through the concerns in the second category and convert "What if?" into "How can I?" For instance, if your fear is, "What if I forget core points during my presentation?" ask yourself, "How can I prepare better?" This makes your worries productive.

Hack 116: Schedule "Worry Time."

As we have seen, constructive concerns can give you ideas and help you prepare. Since humans are hardwired to worry because it ensures their survival, schedule some "worry time." Allot 30 minutes. Don't exceed the limit, and every time you catch yourself worrying other than during the designated period, work on something else. Treat this time as self-care because it is about paying attention to your concerns and finding solutions. The key is to manage worrying as opposed to getting paralyzed by it.

Hack 117: Talk It Through:

Worrying can have you going around in a mental loop, especially if you are alone. In such moments, it helps to reach out to a friend – a fresh pair of ears and another mind. Sometimes, all you need is to let it out because that makes acceptance easier. Empathy and love lead to better mental health and problem-solving. Talking to a compassionate friend will help you sort out your issues effectively. In the case of excessive worrying, you can seek a therapist who can help you manage your stress.

Hack 118: Avoid Suppressing Worries:

The most common advice one receives is, "Don't worry." Sometimes, people think that burying negative thoughts will make them go away. Wishing worries away makes them return with vigor. It is crucial to acknowledge them and move on, as opposed to denying and letting them fester. Research shows that individuals who are more accepting of intrusive thoughts exhibit lower levels of depression and anxiety. Therefore, acknowledge intrusive thoughts and let go.

Hack 119: Uncertainty Is the Only Certainty:

It is crucial to make peace with change because we know little to nothing about what the future holds. Accepting that nothing is permanent will help reduce anxiety. Prepare for different possibilities, if you must, by making plans and being confident about your coping mechanisms instead of having expectations.

Hack 120: Be Mindful, and Here's How:

Mindfulness means being aware of yourself and your surroundings. Mindful meditation is used to alleviate stress and anxiety by directing your attention elsewhere when you're plagued with negative thoughts.

To put it into practice, follow these steps:

- Practice paying attention to your body and its sensations. For instance, the flavor of your toothpaste while brushing your teeth. Try to live in the moment and experience life's simple pleasures.
- Accept yourself wholeheartedly, warts and all. Believe that you are unique and valuable. Focus on your breathing for at least two minutes every day.
- After you have practiced the above, regularly perform a body scan, along with sitting or walking meditations to lighten your mind and body. Sitting meditation is essentially lying on your back with extended limbs and palms facing up. Or, sit comfortably on the floor with folded legs and breathing in and out. Focus on each part of the body and feel the sensations. Similarly, choose a quiet spot of about 20 feet for a walking meditation and walk across it while intensely focusing on the sensations.

39

BEING SPONTANEOUS

"Our spontaneous action is always the best. You cannot, with your best deliberation and heed, come so close to any question as your spontaneous glance shall bring you."
– Ralph Waldo Emerson

Living in the present moment is a gateway into our highest joy. In these bleak times of the pandemic, spontaneity is one of the easiest ways to unlatch the gate. When was the last time you took a trip without planning? Should you be spontaneous? The answer is a resounding 'Yes'!

Let's begin by understanding the concept better: The dictionary defines spontaneity as acting without a lot of planning or thought. It can be misconstrued as rashness or foolishness, but that's not what I am advocating here. My argument is that we must listen to our inner urgings, which are closely connected to our intuition, once in a while. By following the small voice in our hearts, we are led towards our highest good.

The Benefits of Spontaneity:

By reclaiming our freedom of spontaneous expression from the kind of rigid self-control and over-rationalization that stunts growth, we are rewarded with the following:

- **Creativity:** Life coaches say that spontaneous activities enhance intuition and creativity. Both are crucial for career advancement and emotional intelligence.
- **Well-being:** Being open to new, unplanned experiences makes you lighthearted. Dragging yourself from one scheduled activity to the next will make you numb, fatigued, and bored.

- **Curiosity and awe:** As we discussed earlier, most adults plan everything and live in autopilot mode. Acting spontaneously increases curiosity and a sense of wonderment. It appeals to your inner child and helps you come out of your comfort zone. Learning stops the minute you get comfortable in your career or life. Take at least one spontaneous step every week. For instance, volunteer at a local hospital or sign up for a rural internship. This will also teach you a thing or two about yourself.
- **Flexibility and resilience:** If you have these spur-of-the-moment experiences, you will become better at facing challenges. If you periodically choose to break patterns, you will also increase your resilience. Both traits are highly valued across all business sectors. They will be the making of an individual who is willing to expand, grow, and take risks.
- **Delight, cheerfulness, joy:** Pleasant surprises release happy hormones in the brain. They also foster trust, joy, and connection. For instance, to make your colleague's day better, leave some chocolates on their desk, or consider helping a stranger as the following story illustrates:

"My kids and I were heading to the superstore. On the way, we spotted a man wrapped in a blanket and holding a sign that said, 'Lost my job. Family to feed.' At this store, a sight like this is not an everyday occurrence. The man was desperate for help. My ten-year-old commented on how bad it must be to have to stand outside in the cold wind. While we were in the store, I asked each of my seven kids to pick something they thought our 'friend' would appreciate. They chose apples, a shrimp cocktail, a sandwich, some cheese, and a bottle of juice.

Then my 17-year-old asked, 'Can we get him a gift card?' I thought about it. We were low on cash ourselves. Well, sometimes, giving from our need instead of our abundance is just what we need to do! We talked about having to do away with some things if we bought a gift card. All the kids piped in, 'That's okay!' 'I'll eat oatmeal all week!' On and on, each child declared something. In their eagerness, they said, 'Hurry, Mom! Let's give him his stuff before he gets too cold and leaves.' We quickly checked out, grabbed a hot cup of coffee, and drove to where our 'friend' was. We handed him the coffee and the bag of food. He lit up and thanked us with watery eyes. When I gave him the gift card, he burst into tears, obviously overwhelmed and grateful. Though I wish we could have done more, I think about how this experience has been such an excellent opportunity for our family. The impact of how it feels to help someone has rippled through them all -- they cannot stop talking about it, and for days now, have been 'scouting' for others we can help! Things would have played out so differently if I had said, 'No, we don't have money to give more.' Stepping up not only helped a brother in need, but it also gave my kids the sweet taste of helping others."

How to Be Spontaneous:

While spontaneity is necessary to grow and thrive, it should not become impulsiveness; make sure you understand the difference. Before you make a spur-of-the-moment decision, consider the pros and cons.

Don't act without thinking. Learn to distinguish between the voice of your intuition and an emotional reaction or rash decision. While you should explore and act on the former, always hit the "pause" button and take time to consider the latter. If something doesn't feel right about a spontaneous decision, even if you don't know why that is, it's best not to move forward – the uneasiness is likely the voice of your intuition warning you.

Spontaneity can also be examined within the framework of improv comedy, where the keys are creativity and inventiveness. While you must be able to improvise, you should also be aware that all choices have consequences. Are you prepared to deal with them? You must have the foresight and smarts to face the challenges that may come with being spontaneous.

Here are a few "baby-step" suggestions that you can take to safely and comfortably develop this trait:

Hack 121: Say Yes, More Often:

> *"Say yes and you'll figure it out afterwards."*
> — Tina Fey

Say yes to things that interest you. For example, attend a seminar outside the scope of your work. You might learn something that opens you to new ideas. Say yes to things that bring you joy, like calling an old friend. Bond over a coffee, vent, or relive memories you shared. A conversation will surely make you feel good.

Hack 122: Resist the Mundane:

Slowly drop humdrum activities from your day, like TV and doom scrolling. Instead, join a book club even if you're not a voracious reader. Spontaneity is about breaking routines.

Hack 123: Just Do It:

Stop daydreaming about this or that exciting thing. Act spontaneously at least once a week. It could be as simple as a walk in the park or as adventurous as a trip to Goa.

Hack 124: Take Calculated Risks:

Foster growth by getting out of your comfort zone and challenging yourself. Take at least one risk a month, like investing a small sum in a new stock.

Hack 125: Break Rules:

Break the rules without infringing on someone else's rights. If there's a chance that you can experience something new, then do so. For example, it would be harmless if you finished your work quickly and spent your spare time watching a documentary.

40

BEING STILL

"True intelligence operates silently. Stillness is where creativity and solutions to problems are found."
— *Eckhart Tolle*

As we saw in the first section of this book, "knowing oneself" is the foundation to thriving. You cannot live your life's purpose or in alignment with your highest joy if you don't know who you are and what you want!

The shiny technology at our fingertips is life-changing in good and bad ways. It keeps us focused outward – not even in the real world, but at digital representations. We gradually lose our connection with others and our inner compass.

Our self-awareness contracts in a world that is fraught with hyper-connection and a cacophony of opinions. As a result, there are increased levels of stress and poor mental health among people – Millennials and Gen Z, in particular, because they are more addicted to social media.

They are prone to distractions and operate within a cruel capitalist culture that undermines quietude and emphasizes productivity and hyperactivity. The antidote is silence and stillness, which are typically intertwined. Let's understand what we mean by these two terms.

Silence is an absence of noise and speaking. It is external quietude but also extends to inner silence, the silence of the mind. If you are alone in a quiet room, but your mind is racing, you are not practicing silence. In this context, we mean outward and inward silence.

Similarly, stillness is not only an external condition, like taking a break from your errands. While stillness is the absence of activity, it also means inner peace, silencing the mind and finding your center, meaning the tranquility and detachment of the observer within.

Such states are typically reached during meditation but not necessarily in physical stillness. They can be achieved through Yoga, Qigong, martial arts, or a walk in nature. Here is a personal story to help you understand the concept better.

> *A few years ago, I attended a ten-day Vipassana retreat in Igatpuri near Mumbai. In this retreat, I was not allowed to speak, read, write, or make eye contact with anyone. I was supposed to eat moderate amounts of food and meditate. The retreat helped people introspect, allowing them to observe themselves and their thoughts. It ensured that they were disciplined, silent, and mindful for a while. The first three days were uncomfortable because I was trying something new and experiencing a noise detox. Over the next three days, I adjusted to the practices. The last four days were smooth. I became used to the 'inner space.' I was able to resolve my frustration and judgments. During this retreat, I truly learned about the power of silence.*

The Benefits of Stillness and Silence:

As already mentioned, mental health is the greatest benefit of practicing silence and stillness, but there are many more.

- **Self-awareness:** Stillness helps you connect with your true self. It helps you differentiate between the facade you put on for society and the real you. It enables you to focus on your inner world to learn what makes you happy and be grateful.
- **Perspective:** Author Michael Hyatt states that one needs peace and quiet to gain perspective. When you don't make time to be still, you are reactive and influenced by external demands.
- **Stress reduction:** Practicing silence and stillness reduces stress, increases happiness, boosts creativity, improves memory and sleep, etc. It also alleviates anxiety.
- **Patience and acceptance:** When you look at a challenging situation from the detached observer's perspective, you start to see the bigger picture. As a result, your patience and acceptance increase. You learn to let go of things more smoothly.
- **Intuition:** Your intuitive sense is drowned out by mind chatter. The more you shut out the distractions, the more you can tune in to that "small inner voice" and make the most of its invaluable guidance and insight.
- **Improved listening and clarity:** Stillness will teach you to be comfortable with silence, making you a better listener. It also offers clarity.

If you're particularly troubled by a situation and cannot stop thinking about it, a few minutes of silence will calm you and help you find solutions. Here's another story to help you understand better:

> *"A farmer had a watch that was very dear to him. One day, while working in a barn, he lost it in the hay. He looked for it for hours but couldn't find it. Exhausted, he asked the children playing outside to help him, promising a handsome reward. The kids began looking through stacks of hay. One by one, they gave up. The farmer lost hope and called off the search. Just as he was closing the barn door, a little boy requested another chance.*
> *The farmer let the boy inside.*
> *After a while, the boy came out with the watch. Elated, the farmer asked how he had succeeded in finding it while everyone else had failed. The boy replied, 'I just sat there and tried listening for*
> *the ticking. In silence, it was much easier to hear it and search in the direction of the sound.' The farmer rewarded the little boy as promised."*

How to Practice Stillness and Silence:

The takeaway from the above story is that the mind works better in silence, free of distractions. However, staying still and quiet, even for five minutes, can be challenging for some people. If you do not know how to get yourself into a meditative state, here are a few tips to get you started:

- **Designate a spot:** By doing so, you form an association between that place and that state of mind, making the process easier with practice. The prerequisite is that the spot is quiet.
  If you live close to nature, then sitting by the lake or beach is ideal. If you must take time at home, then your study or garden could be perfect. You can even hang a "Do Not Disturb" sign to avoid interruptions.
- **Relax your body:** Sit comfortably on a sofa or recliner. Scan your body for spots where you hold tension. Start at the feet and make your way to the top of your head. Let go of tension by mentally telling that body part to do so or by tensing it up, holding for a few seconds, and releasing.
- **Relax your mind:** Once the body is relaxed, do your best to still your thoughts. There are many helpful techniques, so practice until you discover which one works best for you.
  For example, you can focus on the sensations in your body or on your breath. Or you can listen to calming sounds, meditation music, or binaural beats that induce specific brainwave patterns.

- **Stay in the moment:** Avoid thinking about the past or the future. When random thoughts pop in – and they most certainly will – practice non-judgmental observation. Let them go without indulging them.
  To make the process easier, go mentally to a place that you enjoy, for instance, a beach you fell in love with during a vacation. Think of that moment and recreate that picture and feeling in your mind.

Once you know how to access that still, silent place within, you can practice anywhere and anytime. It could be in a park or taxi. You could do it in your office in the middle of a busy day when you need a few minutes of calm. Here are a few hacks that you can implement:

Hack 126: Increase Stillness and Reduce Distractions:

Begin by scheduling stillness time, a few minutes first thing in the morning before your prayers, exercise, or breakfast. Do your best to increase that time on a daily basis. Also, gradually reduce the time you spend around external stimuli, like screens for entertainment purposes. Set limits and stick to them.

Hack 127: Speak Less:

Avoid speaking unless necessary, especially about insignificant things. Consciously practice being quiet for at least 20 minutes a day. Before bed, spend at least 15 minutes quietly doing and thinking nothing. This helps reduce the chatter in your mind and ensures you fall asleep quickly.

Hack 128: Take Up a Regular Meditative Practice:

Whether that means meditation, Yoga, Tai Chi, or going for a hike, set aside a time when you can go inward. This will help you de-stress, giving you plenty of time to introspect.

Hack 129: Breathe:

A critical component in calming the body and mind is breathing, especially during stressful moments. Take slow, deep breaths to slow your heart rate – this works well if you experience anxiety.

41

MAKING A DIFFERENCE

"How wonderful it is that nobody need wait a single moment before starting to improve the world." – Anne Frank

Many have almost lost hope and feel unmotivated to do anything worthwhile with all that's going on in the world. However, time waits for none. So, instead of sulking, let's gear up for a better tomorrow, where we can thrive individually and collectively since existence is an exercise in symbiosis. Gandhi said, *"You must be the change you wish to see in the world."* As you improve yourself, actualizing more of your potential, you automatically become a beacon of inspiration, empowerment, and change for those around you. You make a difference inadvertently, simply by expressing your kindness, wisdom, and talents.

Motivational speakers like Eric Thomas, Tony Robbins, Les Brown, Jim Rohn, Robin Sharma, or anyone for that matter, emphasize viewing life through a broader lens. In an article in *Forbes,* Margie Warrell published research confirming that people with a purpose greater than themselves are "happier, more contented, and satisfied with life."

Imagine the sense of purpose and fulfillment that drives the people in the following stories, sourced from the website *Life Beyond Numbers*. Dr. Ruma Bhargava and Dr. Megha Bhargava have touched the lives of around 10,500 children in 41 schools in rural India in four years; the sister duo has distributed about 2.5 million meals to the impoverished during the COVID-19 lockdown.

Aditya Prakash Bhardwaj is said to have fed 5,000 during the lockdown, while Pushpa Preeya from Bengaluru has written 700+ exams for the disabled and needy in the past ten years. So many unsung heroes are taking action every day. "How can I make a difference?" you may wonder.

Without massive resources at your disposal, you may question if anything you do matters actually! To this, I respond with Mother Theresa's words, *"It's not how much we give but how much love we put into giving."*

Intention matters because, in the act of giving, two things are exchanged, resources and energy. The energy comes from your heart. It needs to be genuine, wise, and balanced, for there is a shadow aspect to giving.

The Savior Complex:

Also known as the messiah complex, experts define this as "a psychological construct that makes a person feel the need to save others. This person has a strong tendency to seek people who desperately need help and to assist them, often sacrificing their own needs." As honorable as that mindset appears to be, when helping becomes a compulsion, it is unhealthy for several reasons.

First, if sensible parameters are not set, you can drive yourself into the ground, stretching beyond your emotional, financial, and physical limits.

Second, in the absence of discernment, what you give and how you give may be detrimental to the other person, in addition to yourself. The classic example is the parent desperate to help their child by enabling their addiction. When they are incapable of tough love, they contribute to their child's downward spiral.

Third, compulsive giving is an avoidance mechanism. Psychologists say that the savior complex gives the person an outlet to focus on so they can avoid addressing their own problems. World-changers like Mother Teresa, Mahatma Gandhi, Abraham Lincoln, and Nelson Mandela have taught us that the magic of uplifting the world happens when we heal ourselves.

In the spirit of contribution, I impart the knowledge in this book and close with suggestions on how you can make a difference in the world.

Hack 130: Mind Your Manners:

A nice word or gesture can make someone's day because they feel acknowledged. Whether you smile at a cashier or give your seat to someone on the bus, you uplift and assist in the simplest of ways. As Auliq Ice says, *"Manners and politeness will never become old-fashioned."*

Hack 131: Donate and Share:

In addition to money, you can donate clothing, food, time, skills, books, and so on. The idea is to give or share something useful. The size of the donation does not matter; every drop counts. You never know – others may become inspired to give too.

"Thousands of candles can be lit from a single candle, and the life of the candle will not be shortened," said the Buddha.

Hack 132: Serve and Show Love:

"If you can't feed a hundred people, then feed one," urged Mother Teresa. You can assist a sick neighbor or visit shelters and orphanages – play games with the kids, read to the elders, and serve food to the homeless. Tell people how worthy they are. Remember, most of them are either abandoned or have no family. Assure them that they are not alone and that they can reach out to you. However, always make sure to step up when they need you. Fake promises might worsen the emotional trauma.

Hack 133: Focus on the Good; Do Not Judge:

As previously indicated, a contribution is most impactful when it comes from the heart, both for the one who gives and for the one who receives. Look for the good in others, even if you don't see it clearly at first. Always put yourself in the other person's shoes before judging them. You never know what they have been through. Although the world is filled with negativity, stay positive – this way, you are doubling your gift by giving both material things and hope.

Hack 134: Aim for Long-Term Impact:

I cannot stress the importance of this Chinese proverb enough, *"Give a man a fish; you feed him to fish for a day. Teach him how to fish. You feed him for a lifetime."*

When giving, look for projects with lasting benefits. Yes, it's imperative to send people food and medicine in an emergency; however, your money would transform lives if you bought a goat for a family or helped build a well for clean water in a developing country.

Hack 135: Speak Up:

Change can only take place if enough people raise their voices. If Greta Thunberg had stayed silent, we would not have had the greatest climate strike in history. Other young girls, inspired by Greta, have started measures in their own countries.

The point is, one person can make a difference, but a group can bring about a change. Of course, the goal does not have to be that grand. If a person is being bullied at work, speak up in their defense.

You don't have to be confrontational; subtly point out to the bully that their behavior is inappropriate. For example, you can say, "Hey, I felt uncomfortable about how you spoke to that person."

Hack 136: One Small Act of Kindness a Day:

"Three things in human life are important. The first is to be kind. The second is to be kind. And the third is to be kind," Henry James sums up so perfectly. Here are a few things you can practice to make compassion your default setting:

- Do your best not to get angry with people. Never insult them; if you must give critical feedback, make sure it's constructive and expressed with respect. Everybody makes mistakes, even you!
- If someone asks for help, give them a hand. Build up your good karma credits.
- If you hold a high position in society, stay humble. Talk to people; let them know they can reach out to you in times of need.
- Be sociable and approachable; this is an ecosystem. *"You can be, should be, and need to be involved in the world. It truly needs you,"* writes Elaine N. Aron. Being involved does not mean interfering in other people's lives. It means making yourself available, open, and receptive. If they need your opinion, a shoulder to cry on, or an ear to listen, they can reach out to you.
- Strive to be a role model, especially for youth. Teach by example and practice what you preach. Start changing yourself to see the ripple effect around you.

You have reached the end of the book. To help you further, here's a list of all the hacks we previously discussed in the book. These hacks summarize the book. If you are low on time, just give these hacks a read!

Hack 1: Exercise to Discover Your Life Purpose:

Get a pen and a piece of paper, and then set aside some alone time. Start by getting into a relaxed state, like going for a walk or meditating. The goal is to reduce the mind chatter and open up to deeper insights. When you feel centered, write each question at the top of the page, then jot down any answer that comes to mind. Don't worry if you can't answer fully or if the answer doesn't immediately make sense – this is not a race but a process. It may take several sessions before the picture starts to become clear.

a) **Which five adjectives would you use to define success?**
   Complete the sentence in this way, "I am successful if I am/feel..." (e.g., peaceful, rich, attractive, respected, loved). Try not to rationalize or respond based on expectations, either yours or other people's—answer from your gut, feelings, and desires. By exploring your definition of success, you are essentially discovering your version of happiness, which is tied to your life purpose.

b) **Why are these five conditions important to you?**
   Once you have defined what success means to you, the next step is to analyze why you feel this way. If one answer was "I am successful if I am rich," delve into how that idea was created. Did you grow up poor? Don't you have enough disposable income for luxuries? Do you want to be free of the 9-5 grind to travel? If you answer honestly, you will begin to see what you truly value. Only by acknowledging your innermost needs and desires can you discover your purpose.

c) **If you could live your life as another person, who would it be and why?**
   A more indirect approach to the above questions makes it easier to bypass subconscious conditioning. Since this is an imaginary scenario, you are more likely to allow your true desires to surface. If you said, "I would like to be Beyoncé," delve into 'why.' It truly does not matter what Beyoncé's life is actually like. The only thing that matters is how you imagine it and why. Do you have an unfulfilled dream to sing? Do you want to be in the spotlight?

d) **At the end of your life, what things would you wish you had accomplished?**
   Start by writing down your list of desired accomplishments, then switch perspective and ask, "Which three will still be meaningful to me at the end of my life?" For example, you are more likely to realize that spending time with loved ones was more fulfilling than accumulating wealth. Delve deeper by shifting perspective again, "If I continue living my life this way, what three things am I likely to regret on my death bed?"

e) **If someone were to write a book about you, what would you want your story to be?**
Dream big! Make it as grand as possible, "a pioneer explorer; discovered the cure for cancer; among the most gifted filmmakers of all time." The exercise will help you identify the things you wish to be remembered for, your legacy. However, your contribution to the world can be as simple and profound as, "A person who showed love, kindness, and generosity to everyone who crossed their path."

Hack 2: Choose a Life-Spanning Goal:

Remember, this vision is aspirational. Ideally, it should give you a purpose for your whole life, perhaps even inspire others beyond your lifetime.

Hack 3: Choose Something Scary and Exciting:

If it's not daunting, you're thinking too small. If it's not exciting, you won't be able to keep working towards this goal for decades.

Hack 4: Choose Something That Fills You with Energy and Personal Power:

It should get you out of bed every morning. If it doesn't fill you with enthusiasm, then go back to the drawing board. Your vision should invigorate you enough to overcome obstacles and challenges because there will be plenty. You will need to get up, dust yourself off, and carry on.

Hack 5: Choose a Role Model:

You don't need to reinvent the wheel. There are many studies outlining what makes some people extraordinarily successful. Malcolm Gladwell's book Outliers: The Story of Success offers an excellent compilation.

The following exercise will help you choose your role model:
Make a list of three people you admire. List three aspects of each person that make you admire them. Rank these nine aspects in the order of importance (for you). Pick the three that you feel are most important to you. Use these three qualities/aspects in one positive sentence to define your initial desire. Re-write this goal statement in your own words. Keep repeating and tweaking it until it feels aligned. Once you feel good about it, try it out with family and friends. When we say things aloud, they often feel quite different. Tweak and test until you settle on your goal. Give yourself permission to change it if you find that it's not right for you at some point.

Hack 6: Gain Clarity on Why You Want Something:

Find solitude and think, really think, especially before bed. Your subconscious will bring you insights during dreamtime.

The goal of this exercise is to come up with five reasons why you want that life vision. Write it over and over again. Make it yours. Here is an example:

I want to be a musician because...
- I have loved singing ever since I can remember. I want to create music that mesmerizes the audience.
- I can reach millions of people with my message. Music is my way of conveying happiness, sadness, and true feelings to the world.
- Music is the highest form of creative expression for me, and I want to master it.
- Music is pure and speaks directly to the heart

Hack 7: Set SMART Goals:

In Attitude Is Everything: If You Want to Succeed Above and Beyond, Paul J. Meyer describes a system for setting goals he calls 'SMART,' the acronym for Specific, Measurable, Achievable, Relevant, Time-bound. Let's get a better understanding.

- Specific: Your goal should be clear and specific; otherwise, you won't be able to focus your efforts. When drafting your goal, answer the following questions:
- What do I want to accomplish? Why is this goal important? Who is involved? Which resources are required? What are the limits?
- Measurable: Assessing your progress helps you meet deadlines and stay motivated. If your goal is measurable, you should be able to answer such questions: How much? How many? How will I know when it is accomplished?
- Achievable: To determine whether a goal is attainable, answer the following questions: How can I accomplish this goal? How realistic is it considering the various constraints?
- Relevant: This step ensures that the goal aligns with your roadmap and grand vision for your life. If it is, you should be able to answer 'yes' to such questions: Does it seem worthwhile? Is this the right time? Does this complement my other efforts/needs? Am I the right person to reach this goal? Is it applicable in the current socio-economic environment?

- Time-bound: Every goal needs a target date to prevent postponement and delays. You should be able to answer these questions: When is the earliest I can achieve this? What can I do to move forward today? What can I do six weeks from now? What can I do six months from now?

Hack 8: Objectives and Key Results (OKR):

This framework helps organizations define objectives and track results. The concept was created by Andy Grove, popularized by John Doerr, and used in Google, LinkedIn, Twitter, Dropbox, Spotify, Airbnb, and Uber. It is based on finding measurable and verifiable markers for lofty goals and can be applied to one's personal life. Set the objective (what you want to accomplish) and the key results (how you will achieve it).

Hack 9: Have an Accountability Partner:

Find someone you respect who is equally goal-oriented – a mentor, life coach, or friend. Discuss your progress regularly – talking about your goals makes your KRs more tangible and keeps you motivated.

Hack 10: The Fundamentals:

The following conditions are prerequisites to the flow state:

- Acting on your passion. You can only reach a flow state when you are doing something you genuinely enjoy.
- Acting on your talents. The activity should also be something you are good at and in alignment with who you are.
- Just challenging enough. The task should not be overly easy or difficult. It should present a challenge but be well within your capabilities.
- Focusing on the journey, not the result. To borrow another example from sport, this can be described as a runner concentrating on his race and not the gold medal.

Hack 11: How to Get in The Flow?

The following things can help you reach this state more often or regularly:
- No distractions: Eliminate as many of the things that disturb and distract you as possible. Find a quiet place to work, put your phone away, try a website blocker, etc.

- Create a ritual: A meditation, a short walk, a pot of tea, or music can help calm the so-called "monkey mind" and put you in the mood. The ritual conditions your mind to prepare for that state. The more you do it, the easier it gets.
- Keep a journal: Observing conditions and recording your responses is especially helpful when you are learning to get in the flow. Begin by identifying the times when your mind most naturally functions at full speed. Note changes to your ritual and their respective results.
- Mono-task the most important assignment: The flow state is reached while focusing on something that requires significant brainpower. Multitasking creates distractions, which make it impossible to get into the flow. Focus on the day's main task during your most productive time.

Hack 12: Manifestation Practices and Tools:

Although this is not an exhaustive list, the following suggestions will help you use the LOA more effectively:

- **Daydreams, Visualizations:** When you decide what you want to attract into your reality, imagine the desired outcome in detail and often. Make-believe that it has already manifested feeling those emotions as genuinely and as long as possible.
- **Affirmations, Hypnosis:** Our mindsets start being programmed into our subconscious minds in childhood. If your parents were always saying, "We don't have enough," lacking becomes your default. By repeating an affirmation like, "I have enough," you overwrite the default program, actually creating new neuropathways in your brain. Hypnosis speeds up the process.
- **Phrasing:** The affirmation "I will be rich someday" defers the manifestation to the future. Rephrasing it to "I am rich" or "How did I get rich so quickly?" instructs the universe to create that reality as soon as possible. Also, the LOA registers negative statements like "I don't want to be poor" as "poor," reinforcing the very thing that you don't want because you are focused on the fear of poverty, not the joy of prosperity.
- **Thought-control:** When you have a problem, work on solutions without fixating on negative scenarios. Do not hold onto the energy of the problem in your "creation vortex" by thinking about it constantly.
  When fearful thoughts come, say, "No, I will not think about that," and distract yourself with something positive.

- **Resistance:** Often, even when we do all the right things, the manifestation fails – this indicates that resistance is keeping us in a negative vibration. Try soul-searching through journaling, psychoanalysis, guided meditation, or conversation with a trusted friend.

Hack 13: Raising Your Vibration:

The LAO responds to how you feel more powerful, quick, and efficient than your thoughts and words, and it cannot be fooled. If you say, "I feel confident," when you are fearful, the manifestation will match your feelings, not your words. So, the key is managing your emotions and raising your vibration.

How? Deliberately and gradually. For example, do not suppress your fear; it is perfectly natural and needs to be expressed. Suppressing it will only create resistance.

Give yourself some time to feel uneasy but do not wallow in it. As soon as possible, reach for a better feeling by playing with your pet, for example. By engaging in joyful activities and thoughts, you can deliberately raise your vibration bit by bit, moving from feelings of limitation to empowerment.

According to the Abraham-Hicks teachings, the scale from the lowest to the highest emotional resonance is as follows: Fear-despair-grief-depression, guilt-unworthiness; hatred-rage, revenge, anger, worry, frustration, contentment, optimism, enthusiasm, love-joy-gratitude.

Hack 14: Program Your Subconscious:

- Stop the negative programming. Mainstream media is one of the biggest sources of stress in our daily lives; it may not appear that way because we are so used to listening to the prophets of doom 24/7, but you will feel the difference when you disconnect from their constant poisoning. Also, limit the time you spend with pessimistic people because they inadvertently reinforce the programming you aim to break.
- Begin the positive programming. Use affirmations to program your subconscious for abundance – this works only by repetition, meaning changing your self-talk from negative to positive.
  For example, **instead of thinking,** "I don't have enough money," **keep telling yourself,** "I am earning more and more every day." To speed up the process, consider using recorded abundance affirmations (while you sleep, for example) to imprint new thought patterns in your mind. At the same time, form friendships with people with a positive outlook.

Hack 15: Manifest through intention, not by default:

The Law of Attraction says that what you think about becomes your reality. When our thoughts are focused on what we don't have, we manifest lack by default because life reflects us precisely what we think about, like "a self-fulfilling prophecy." The key is to manifest consciously through intention and acting accordingly.

Hack 16: Look to the future:

Become inspired by people who spread hope based on real science and projections, like the Futurists. The ones I follow closely are:

- Ray Kurtzweil is one of the leading Futurists of our time. More than 80% of his predictions have come true on or ahead of his predicted date. At present, his most prominent prediction is, "By 2029, computers will have human-level intelligence."
- Peter Diamandis, a co-founder of Singularity University with Ray Kurtzweil, is a visionary interested in space exploration. One of his recent predictions is that by 2025, the IoE will exceed 100 billion connected devices, each with a dozen or more sensors collecting data.
- Thomas Frey's predictions include, "By 2030, the average person in the U.S. will have 4.5 packages a week delivered with flying drones. They will travel 40% of the time in a driverless car, use a 3D printer to print hyper-individualized meals, and will spend most of their leisure time on an activity that hasn't been invented yet."
- Dave Asprey is more of a bio-hacker, aiming to live to 180 through various methods, many of which are already being adopted by millions.

Hack 17: Use Tools, and Keep Them Handy:

Ideas and thoughts are mercurial, here one moment, gone the next. Unless you write them down quickly, they will slip away. Make use of the following tools and methods:

- **Create an idea journal:** Buy a small notebook and jot down your ideas immediately. I prefer a notebook to an app because we remember better when we write things down. Keep a waterproof pad and pen handy if you have ideas in the shower. If you come up with ideas just before bed, keep your journal on your nightstand.

- **Anywhere, anytime:** How many times have we heard about people jotting down brilliant ideas on a napkin at a coffee shop? The rule of thumb is, scribble it down on anything, anywhere, immediately. Don't wait until you get home.
    o **Use apps:** If you're glued to your phone, you may prefer curating your ideas using apps like Evernote or Google Notes, which can be linked to your calendar.

Here's a list of other excellent tools:
- Milanotes
- Diaro
- Trello
- Feedly… and many more.

Hack 18: Use Productivity Tools:

Tools like RescueTime or a simple timer can stop you from losing track of time, over-committing, or under-committing to a task.

Hack 19: Say 'NO':

People often think that they are more productive when they fill their day with all kinds of things. What ends up happening is that they are overwhelmed, and the work is of low quality. Don't take on more than you can handle. Say 'no' to things that are unimportant or demand too much from you. You may want to seize every opportunity, but make sure that it's aligned with your goals.

Hack 20: Rise Early:

Everyone is always complaining that there aren't enough hours in the day. Why not add a couple? Early birds catch the worm. For instance, wake up at 6 AM, spend time journaling, reading, and making to-do lists before starting your day. Do this for a month and see the difference in your productivity levels.

Hack 21: Use Your Commute:

If you travel to work, or anywhere for that matter, use it by listening to podcasts or audiobooks. You will learn a great deal, from improved vocabulary to new ideas. You can also make important calls to save time.

Hack 22: Social Media Detox:

On average, people spend more than two hours on social media sites like Twitter and Instagram. Limit the use of these apps. Spend that time reading a book or watching an informative documentary.

Hack 23: Automate, Delegate, and Eliminate:

Look for faster ways of completing tasks without compromising quality. Speed up tasks using software. For example, use Grammarly to check spelling and grammar in your documents. Delegate. For instance, give a trusted colleague the task of fact-checking a presentation rather than doing it yourself. Eliminate time-consuming tasks and redundant communication. Reduce the number of items to be discussed in meetings to the crucial ones. Eliminate fluff; keep your communications as precise and brief as possible.

Hack 24: The Integrity Checklist:

In an article for Success, Robin Amster lists the following steps to cultivating integrity:

- Fulfill your promises and keep all appointments. Think carefully before making a commitment. Be realistic about your promises. Say "no," and be comfortable with it. You can't do it all, and that's OK. Always introspect and examine your knee-jerk reactions. What are they signaling?
- Work on fixing your malicious behavior and poor manners. Develop effective and confident communication to avoid misunderstandings. Avoid people who lack integrity.

Hack 25: Say What You Mean, Do What You Say:

If you are unsure whether you can keep your word, it's always best to admit it up front. Never allow yourself to think that you can refuse to do what you have promised. Be honest and clear from the start. Avoid sugarcoating feedback or opinions. Be precise and straightforward.

Hack 26: Be Accountable:

There may be occasions when you mess up. You may not be able to go through with something because of a mistake or emergency. Take responsibility in times like these. Offer to clean up the mess. Accountability is crucial at all times on both personal and professional fronts.

Hack 27: Surround Yourself with People Who Value and Practice Integrity:

We are defined by the company we keep because our friends have a big influence on our lives. To cultivate integrity, socialize with people who have the trait. Avoid mindless gossip and indulge in healthy, meaningful conversations.

Hack 28: Focus on The Small Things; The Larger Ones Will Sort Themselves Out:

By focusing on the small but significant things that you can control, you can cultivate integrity. For instance, if you want your team to perform well in a project, instead of worrying and whining, do your part well. Even if the project does not meet the ideal standard, your effort will be seen and valued.

Hack 29: Use the 3 Rs:

As given by James Clear, the 3 Rs of creating good habits are: remind, routine, reward. Use reminders (e.g., on your devices) to do the required action.

The action needs to be done at a particular time every day, thereby making it a routine. Finally, reward yourself for the effort. After a successful week of eating healthy, treat yourself to dessert on Sunday.

Hack 30: Set a Daily Routine:

Routines help you prioritize your tasks and stay focused. This is especially helpful if you tend to procrastinate.

You can have 2-3 daily routines:
- Morning routine to get the best possible start to the day; a routine after you return from work; a night routine that might include reflecting on your day. Did you get the most important things done? If something wasn't done, decide whether it is still vital. If yes, schedule it for the next day.

Hack 31: It's Easier to Replace Than Eliminate:

Rather than trying to eliminate a bad habit, replace it with a good one. Select the behavior you want to change and decide what to do instead. For example, a friend who loves singing wanted to stop smoking. Every time she was tempted to pick up a cigarette, she would pick up her guitar and sing.

Hack 32: Have an Accountability Partner:

Ask someone you trust and respect to hold you accountable for the changes you want to make in your life. This will add positive pressure, compelling you to stick to your commitment every day. It is also rewarding to receive positive affirmation from a friend.

Hack 33: How to Speak Mindfully:

These tips will help you control the tendency to speak carelessly, make you a better conversation partner and someone people want to interact with, and do wonders for your personal and professional life.

- Know your audience. You would not discuss quantum mechanics with a child. Understand your conversation partner and cater to their needs. Put yourself in the other person's shoes. Be mindful of the other person's situation. Don't boast about luxuries in front of someone who is struggling to make ends meet.
- Listen. Always respond to what the person has said; this makes for effective dialogue. Many people are in a rush to speak, wanting to control the conversation. However, the one who listens has the advantage because they are aware of all points made. Listen 80% of the time, and speak 20%. Make people feel special. Make a habit of acknowledging people's efforts, using positive phrases like "I'm proud of you," "You deserve this, and more."

Another way of making someone feel special is by addressing them with their names, especially in large meetings and groups.

- Know your place. Before making any comments, make sure that you have the right to speak about the matter and that your input was requested. Stay positive: If you are always whining, you spread negativity. Instead of saying to yourself or other people, "I doubt we can do it," say, "We will do it." Use your words to promote harmony, kindness, peace, and a friendly environment.
- Offer support and encouragement. Your words should help others choose the right path, reminding them of their goodness. When angry, hold your tongue. Silence heals. Even if someone is shouting at you, keep silent and listen. Reflect on your response, asking yourself, "Is what I want to say truthful and beneficial? Am I the right person to say it? Is this the right time?" As the father of our nation rightly said, "Speak only if it improves upon the silence."

Hack 34: Timeless Wisdom:

The Bhagavad Gita teaches self-inquiry and transformative action rather than responding heatedly at the moment:
- Self-awareness. Notice not only what you say but also how you say it. Ask yourself, "How do I feel after certain remarks? How do the recipients of those remarks react?"
- Self-inquiry. If you often feel compelled to say hurtful or derogatory things, ask, "What makes me say what I say? What emotions am I suppressing? Is what I'm saying true? How can I deal with this situation without harsh words?"

Hack 35: The Attraction Cheat-Sheet:

The following body language signs will help you ascertain whether people are attracted to you. When someone finds you appealing and engaging:

They lean in, they tilt their head while talking to you, they smile at you, they make eye contact with you, they observe and attentively listen to you.

Of course, you can signal to other people that you find them engaging by using the same body language, making you more attractive. Everyone enjoys being appreciated.

Hack 36: Brush Up on Your Manners and Etiquette:

Even your manners and etiquette are up to par, ensure that you are keeping up with the times. Adhere to other cultures' social norms and customs, especially if you are doing business with people from other countries. Learn things such as politically correct terminology, greetings, pronoun use, gifting, tipping, formalities, etc.

Hack 37: Personality Development Classes:

These courses teach you to identify your weaknesses and strengths. They help you become the best version of yourself. Whether you are starting from scratch or want to polish yourself, they can be useful.

Hack 38: Play by the Rule:

The 70/30 rule, as defined by Jim Rohn, is a good habit to adopt. After paying taxes, 70% of your income needs to go to expenditures. The remaining 30% needs to be divided into three parts and allocated to capital investment, charity, and savings. Adopt this method every month to save more, earn from your wealth, and give back to the community.

Hack 39: Access All Available Resources:

You do not have to study economics or be an investment manager to manage and invest your money.

- In the Internet age, educating yourself on how money works has never been easier. You can access endless resources, either inexpensively or free of charge – books, courses, lectures, etc. Keep in mind, however, that the learning never stops.
- If you cannot hire a personal finance manager yet, you can access free information and advice from sources like local banks. Make an appointment with a bank-level financial advisor and ask questions. See what investments they have to offer. With that said, banks will only offer their products, which may not be the most competitive or lucrative on the market. Even if you buy a term deposit for six months, your money will be earning something while you shop around for a better rate.
- Use technology to manage your wealth in a hassle-free and effective manner. Apps can help you budget and invest on a single device. Your financial information is no longer stored in reams of paper.

Hack 40: Avoid Debt Like the Plague:

Buying on credit isn't very smart. Shop with cash and debit cards only. If you cannot repay the full amount of your credit card balance, then cancel it or pay it off and set it aside for a rainy day.

Hack 41: Invest First; Spend Later:

Make your investments and savings monthly and automatic. Invest in equities but be prepared to remain in the game for years.

Hack 42: Avoid Withdrawing Retirement Funds:

Make it difficult to withdraw from your retirement fund by placing it in long-term fixed deposits. Choose annuities that are illiquid and offer substantial income.

Hack 43: Spend Less; Keep More:

- Buy fewer things and only what you absolutely need.
- Buy second-hand items whenever you can.

- Purchase major assets based on needs, not as status symbols. Sell them if there is a risk of them becoming a liability.
- Sell big assets you do not regularly use (e.g., car, boat, vacation home) and invest the money where you can yield high returns.
- Choose profit income liquidity over setting up a business.

Hack 44: Share More; Earn More:

- Earn extra income from under-utilized skills.
- Rent out spare rooms or second homes.
- If you own a car, earn by freelancing on Uber as a driver on weekends or days convenient to you.

Hack 45: Mind the Pitfalls:

It's crucial to use technology to save money as long as you are mindful of the following:

- Online stores make shopping super easy and tempting. Before making a purchase, make sure that this is something you truly need or want. Beware of clickbait and relentless advertising. Try not to fall for it. Run specific searches only for things you need. Once you have all the information, unsubscribe from promotional emails, or you will be inundated with emails, ads, suggestions, etc.

Hack 46: Don't Sell Yourself Short:

If you think you deserve a raise at work, ask for it. The worst that can happen is that you won't get it. If you are running a freelance business, start raising your hourly rates when you have enough ongoing clients.

Hack 47: Upskill and Offer Exceptional Service:

It's critical to leverage your current employment situation fully. Always focus on creating value for the company you work for, and the money will follow.

Hack 48: Make Your Money Earn:

Start with simple things like switching to a savings account that pays you the highest interest on deposits. Invest as much as you can. Avoid withdrawing from your investments and make it a rule to only add to them.

Hack 49: Create Active Income Streams:

Take side-gigs but be ethical about moonlighting. Also, look for income outside of the skillset that you use in your job. For example, monetize your blog, sell your art, or get involved in e-commerce.

Hack 50: Create Passive Income Streams:

Try to create one new source of passive income every month, like dividend stocks and rentals.

Hack 51: Explore Job Crafting:

Job crafting refers to employees redesigning and reimagining their jobs to increase satisfaction. This is especially useful when you cannot quit a mundane position. Job crafting is usually done by:

- **Changing functions:** For instance, an accountant may devise a better method for filing taxes to reduce repetition and improve efficiency.
- **Shifting peer relationships:** A computer engineer may teach advanced computer skills to a colleague, creating interaction and learning opportunities for both parties. If the engineer enjoys teaching, he can develop tutorials either for his workplace or online.
- **Shifting perspective:** No job is too menial; every role provides value – this cannot be stressed enough! Even if you are not working your dream job, you are contributing to society, or you would not be paid. For example, a hospital janitor may see his role as vital instead of dull because it contributes to patient safety.

Hack 52: Put Good Advice to Practice:

To do well at work, consider the following advice from leaders in the corporate world.

- **Don't be paralyzed by fear:** Take risks, plan, and push yourself to achieve what you can. Know that you're capable of anything. Fear only holds you back, so tame it. To err is human.
- **Manage your career and decide for yourself:** Don't do what others are doing. Listen to criticism with a pinch of salt. Your job needs to be defined based on what you want and not what others have.

- Learn something new every day: Read an article to improve your knowledge or sign up for a course that will help you upskill or make a career shift.
- Never attach your self-worth to your job: Sure, doing well at work improves self-esteem, but knowing that you are not your job is critical. You are of value, irrespective of having a career.

Hack 53: Identify the Area of Your Desired Expertise:

You need to decide what you want to be known for and work towards it. It is usually easier to build on existing knowledge and skills, but that is not to say that you can't develop in a new area. For example, if you are already a good marketing copywriter, you may want to become an SEO expert.

Hack 54: Assess Your Skills and Gain Expertise:

Once you identify what area you want to gain expertise in, do an honest self-assessment.

Are you the best? If not, how can you become the best? Research what the most successful professionals are doing. What can you learn from them? How can you improve your work based on their example? Most importantly, how can you develop your unique approach? How can you make yourself stand out?

Using the information you have gathered, create a plan to achieve your goal of being exceptional. Attend training sessions, upskilling programs, and practice as much as possible.

Hack 55: Keep Proving and Improving Your Expertise:

As already mentioned, keep your employers informed about your accomplishments. Showcase upskills by suggesting and implementing innovative approaches. Soon, your work will show results, and the recognition will begin. If the results aren't satisfactory, find where you're going wrong and fix it.

Hack 56: Habits That Make You a Valuable Employee:

Even if you are not an expert in your field nor wish to be, the following suggestions will increase the value that you bring to your job every day:

- Be proactive. Work ahead of the curve. Foresee problems and solve them effectively. Finish things before the deadline – this allows enough time for revisions, improvements, additions, etc.

- Always make a plan and stick to it. If the situation changes, be flexible.
- Solve problems at their root, avoiding temporary fixes as much as possible.
- Commit only to what is achievable and do it exceptionally well.
- Always fight for what is right.

Hack 57: Adopt and Practice the Four Es:

- **Empathy:** Showing empathy means caring about other people's feelings and treating them with respect and kindness. Put yourself in their shoes, and listen to their concerns. This will not only make you a better person but you will also be perceived as an asset to the firm.
- **Education:** Take the time to educate yourself and your peers without being condescending. Also, educate your customers to help them make the best choice for them – being honest builds trust between buyers and sellers, leading to repeat business. Education also means being informed regarding inclusive language and behavior.
- **Ecosystem:** Being mindful of the ecosystem means creating a work environment that is positive, healthy, and conducive to helping others. Foster the service mindset in your workplace by practicing what you preach – this will encourage others to adopt a generous attitude.
- **Encouragement:** By helping people grow, you help yourself and your company. Recognize the efforts of others. Show your appreciation and motivate them with a nice gesture like buying lunch. Remember that success is a journey that everyone takes together.

Hack 58: Be of Service, Not Servile:

Being servile is a slippery slope that ends in being exploited, losing respect and self-respect, not being taken seriously, even being disliked by people who will view this behavior as disingenuous, cowardly, and desperate. So, how can you apply the Law of Reciprocity in the work environment without being servile?

Look for opportunities to help others. However, make you don't overdo it. For example, during negotiations, ask many questions without being annoying – this makes the other party feel that you care about their project. In the event of a disagreement, agree to the terms slowly and be fair. Make sure you communicate the importance of fairness.

Hack 59: Develop a Service-Oriented Persona:

To do this, you need to adopt and practice the following behaviors until they become personality traits:

- Care and help: Look out for clients and teammates. Help them as much as you can, within reason.
- Make an effort: Go out of your way to deliver the best results and create a positive work environment.
- Make people feel valued: Foster engagement by making your colleagues feel valued. Also, help them socialize.
- Practice what you preach: Teach by example. Take time to mentor juniors and help them grow. At the same time, keep working on yourself.

Hack 60: Ask and Listen:

Knowing how to ask questions and listen is critical in any interaction, even if you are working remotely from home.

- Ask questions – this will force you to listen intently. Do not hesitate to ask for clarification. Delivering work based on a wrong assumption is worse.
- Paraphrase your understanding and repeat it back to the person to ensure you have understood correctly.
- Take a genuine interest in what the person is saying. Most of the time, we wait for the other person to stop talking, so we can jump in with our thoughts.
- While someone is speaking, do not interrupt. Keep all your distractions (phone, email, etc.) away; no multi-tasking.

Hack 61: Surefire Tips to Professional Conduct:

- Be always on guard: When you are in public, and especially at work, operate from the assumption that everyone is carefully watching your actions and reactions – because they are!
- Don't get drawn into unprofessional behaviors: Always speak well of yourself and others. Do not get drawn into gossip, badmouthing, and self-denigration. If people are engaging in such behavior around you, remove yourself from the situation.
- Don't gripe to coworkers: If you have a legitimate complaint, speak to those responsible, the management or HR.

- Be neutral: Be objective and unbiased at all times. Neutrality is easy when you remove yourself from the equation. If you are assembling a team, choose the most capable, not the most pliable. The same goes for solving problems. Your focus should be on finding the best solution, not about personally gaining from the situation.
- Be open to all ideas: Avoid being too attached to your ideas. Do not be envious or resentful if your colleagues come up with better ones. Aim to do what's best for the company.
- Acknowledge everyone's contribution: Even if you were the driving force behind a professional success, do not boast or take all the credit. Give credit where credit is due, and make everyone on the team feel appreciated.
- Spread some cheer: Suggest and implement ways to boost morale. Team lunches and retreats help in creating an upbeat environment at work.
- Maintain your professional comportment outside work: Do not let your guard down or behave immaturely or inappropriately outside the workplace – this includes office parties, work functions, social media, etc. Drunken videos of yourself will undermine your professionalism.
- Avoid the entitled mindset: Regardless of how accomplished you are, stay humble and relevant. No one owes you a living; keep earning your stripes every day on the field. Do not rest on your laurels.

Hack 62: Bond with the Boss:

Building rapport with your superiors is critical to getting noticed. How can you accomplish that subtly and professionally?

- Ensure that you speak to your boss regularly. Meet with them at least once a week for about 10-15 minutes and bring value to these discussions. Keep meetings and conversations at work professional. However, as you start to build rapport with your boss, some personalization is fine. Avoid feigning interest in their life. Also, you don't necessarily have to share details of your personal life.
- Always go fully prepared to meetings and keep conversations crisp. If you have specific points to discuss, make notes, and plan ahead. Give your managers updates and keep them informed of any challenges. Seek their help if you require it. Present your proposals, solutions, and suggestions to your boss. This will not only bring a fresh pair of eyes to your ideas but also encourage collaboration.

Hack 63: Grow Your Network Offline:

How many people do you know outside of your team in your organization? Do you know at least two people in upper management, or are you essentially invisible? If you have no connections or exposure to management, then your chances of being noticed are next to none. You can fix this by:

Making a concerted effort to meet people outside your immediate professional circle at your company and elsewhere. Attend networking events, conferences, conventions, forums, training seminars, etc. Research your company's hierarchy and identify people who can help your career. Connect with them on LinkedIn or in the workplace. At work, you can ask for a meeting if you have something specific to discuss or strike up a conversation with people who can help your career and managers from other teams. For example, break the ice in the cafeteria by commenting on the day's special. Be friendly but brief. Next time you see the person in the hallway, say hello.

Hack 64: Grow Your Network and Cachet Online.

- Use LinkedIn effectively. The platform is built to connect professionals. It helps you get noticed, get jobs, and also showcase your potential. It provides insight into the minds of employers and employees alike. It also gives indications of where your industry is headed and what you can learn to improve. Add your managers, colleagues, and competition as your connections. This will get you noticed for better jobs, collaborations, and projects.
- Build a strong online presence, especially if you are an expert or in the creative field. Recruiters today ask for LinkedIn profiles, and social media handles to get to know their candidates better. You can also create a personal website, which serves as a CV. It goes without saying that you need to keep all your social media accounts looking professional and wholesome.
- Even if you are not an expert or in a creative field, experts suggest getting creative with your resumes, like designing them on your Instagram or Facebook pages.
  You could also create a comprehensive resume using InDesign and supplement it with your LinkedIn profile.
- Showcase your industry knowledge by writing articles and informative posts. Out of sight is out of mind, so ensure that you post regularly. Next time your manager is looking for someone to handle a challenging project on whose theme you write about regularly on social media, they may consider you for the role.

Hack 65: Tips on How to Think Like an Entrepreneur:

- Let your passion guide you. If you don't love your work, then it's time to explore other opportunities. Even if you are not able to change jobs, transfer to another department, reimagine and expand your role.
- Use all resources at your disposal. This can take many forms, like retraining, brainstorming with people with novel perspectives, using new software, etc. If you are running a business, this will take your business to new levels; if you are an employee, your employability and value will increase.
- Find your unique selling proposition. All entrepreneurs and businesses have something that sets them apart. Identify your strengths and leverage them to become a sought-after expert. Do not tolerate mediocrity in yourself or others. If you're an employee, ensure that you do not produce poor or mediocre work. If you are a manager, set a high standard for everyone, including yourself.
- Take calculated risks. Whether you are an employer or employee, you need to take risks to grow without acting impulsively or recklessly. Apply for challenging roles outside your comfort zone. Be smart about it, and take risks that can yield high returns.
- Be goal-oriented. Set attainable short-term and long-term goals and work diligently toward them. If you get stuck, brainstorm with trusted and like-minded colleagues and come up with new approaches. Take initiatives. Entrepreneurs are self-starters. They challenge the status quo by coming up with creative solutions. Being self-motivated and self-directed will set you apart as a leader, not a follower.
- Go beyond your pay. Offer more value for the money by "going above and beyond" – this is especially useful when you are starting out in a new company or career. See this as an investment in yourself because it helps you become the best you can be and indispensable. One approach you can use is asking yourself, "If I were the owner of this firm, how would I solve the problem?" Manage your time and focus.

  Avoid distractions as much as possible, putting time into things that will propel you, like attending networking events rather than chilling with Netflix every night. Be adaptable and future-oriented. Like inventors, when entrepreneurs see a problem, they see an opportunity to develop a solution they can market. They work according to a plan but remain flexible. Adapting to change easily will make you future-oriented rather than stuck in the past.

Hack 66: Be Tech-Savvy:

No matter which role you're in, learn as much as you can. Up-to-date tech skills are beneficial regardless of whether you change jobs or not.

Hack 67: Develop Transferable Skills and Core Competencies:

Things like leadership, communication, creativity, and people skills are sought-after across domains. The more you have, the greater your advantage.

Hack 68: Maintain a Success Journal:

This will come in handy when you ask for a promotion or need to showcase your achievements to a potential employer. It also affirms your strengths and builds your confidence and self-esteem.

Hack 69: Unlearn:

Keep up with the times and let go of obsolete approaches, replacing them with new ones. For instance, if you're a writer, learn about inclusive language so you can leave out outdated, offensive terms from your copy.

Hack 70: Keep Evaluating and Investing in Yourself:

Ask, "What can I do to make myself indispensable or carve out a new path, even within the same company?" For example, when a company automates a few tasks, employees have more time on their hands. Put this time to use by taking up new responsibilities. The chances of you being laid off are lower and getting a promotion higher. It will also give you experience in new areas. Use a percentage of your income to upskill or invest in your business, like buying software that will open up new income streams.

Hack 71: Become a Trouble-Shooter:

Strive to become the company's go-to person when it comes to coming up with solutions – this will make you an invaluable asset.

Hack 72: Become a Mediator:

To avoid conflict, many people tolerate negative situations in the workplace, leaving things to fester. Even if you are not in HR, you can make yourself valuable by mediating. Be objective but also mindful about doing the right thing.

Hack 73: Beware of What You Put into Your Body:

Consume chemical-free food. Buy fresh and organic as often as possible. Wash your vegetables and fruits using hot water with salt and turmeric. With affordable hydroponics kits, you can grow greens and vegetables at home. Drink clean water that is free of fluoride, which is hazardous and can even cause toxicity.

Use natural cosmetic/hygiene products; things like lotions contain harmful substances like parabens, which are absorbed into your skin, the largest organ in the body.

Hack 74: Cleanse and Detoxify:

Since toxins have a long-lasting impact, it is essential not only to limit exposure but also to detoxify. There are many over-the-counter products and home remedies that can help.

Cleanse. Certain herbs, which are not part of the normal diet, help detoxification. There are countless formulations on the market for specific organs and purposes, but the main ones are burdock root, sarsaparilla, dandelion, mullein, bromelain, papain, elderberry, and cilantro.

Food: Increasing intake of cruciferous vegetables, lemon, green tea, garlic, turmeric, chlorella, beets, blueberries, and tomatoes boosts the body's ability to eliminate toxins.

Water: Drinking plenty of water helps flush our toxins daily.

Sweat: Sweat expedites the removal of toxins. Make sure to continuously wipe your skin so as not to reabsorb the toxins.

Sleep: A good night's sleep allows your brain to eliminate toxins.

Hack 75: Mold Exposure:

Consider a urine mycotoxin screen if you think you've been exposed. The following things will help you speed up recovery:

- Avoid moldy foods. According to Dave Asprey, you can speed up recovery by avoiding moldy foods: all grains except white rice; corn, beans, oats, peanuts, cottonseed; cheese; bread; pork (unless pastured); aged meats; all alcohol, but wine and beer are the worst; coffee and chocolate (unless mold-tested); dried fruit; Brazil nuts; pistachios; chili, pre-ground black pepper, and other spices.
- Detox therapies. Infrared saunas, 24-hour fasting, cryotherapy or ice baths, red light therapy, acupuncture, and intravenous vitamin C or glutathione can accelerate recovery.

Hack 76: Health and Wellness Journal:

To take charge of your health and wellness, you need to be aware of your patterns to adjust them. The process involves four steps:

Step 1: Track your daily activities without trying to change your habits. Simply record the following for at least one week:

The number of sleep-hours, bed, and wake-up times. Mealtimes and the food you consume – the percentage of fruits, vegetables, protein, and carbohydrates.

- How much water do you drink per day? How much physical exercise do you get per day?
- How many unhealthy substances do you consume and in what quantities – alcohol, cigarettes, etc.
- How many prescription drugs do you use? How many over-the-counter medications do you use, like painkillers and sleep aids? Height, weight, and Body Mass Index [BMI]. How many hours of negative media do you consume? How much time do you dedicate to a mindfulness practice like meditation, prayer, and introspection? How much time do you spend with your loved ones? How much time do you spend in nature? How much time do you spend doing something that you love, like art or playing music?

Step 2: Analyze the information. Once you've gathered enough data, calculate the averages.

Step 3: Identify the things you need to change. Note all the things that do not contribute to optimum health and divide them into two lists. The first list should include those you can shift fairly easily.

For example, if you are not drinking enough water, bring a water bottle everywhere you go. The second list should include matters that require professional help. For example, if you are taking painkillers for headaches often, find out what is causing the problem by seeing a health practitioner.

Step 4: Take action. Eliminating all unhealthy habits will take time, but "a journey of a thousand miles begins with the first step." To keep motivated, start with a couple of things that you can change easily, like increasing your water intake.

Hack 77: Out of Sight, Out of Mouth:

The first thing you need to do is get rid of all unhealthy foods from your pantry and desk at work. If you can't reach for it, you won't eat it.

Hack 78: Prepare Healthy Snacks Ahead of Time:

We all like to munch on chips and cookies in front of the TV. The way around this is to prepare healthy snacks ahead of time. For example, pre-cut carrots and celery sticks and sprinkle them with lemon juice and a bit of Himalayan salt – this way, you can satisfy your craving for a savory snack while doing something good for your body. Or reach for some seaweed!

Hack 79: Consume Healthy Fats:

Your mother was right; ghee is good for you. Eat lots of healthy fats like avocadoes, nuts, coconut, coconut oil, olives, olive oil, etc. Not only will these do wonders for your body, but they are also very satisfying. Don't overdo it.

Hack 80: Eat Local and Seasonal:

Your grandmother's advice was sound: Whatever grows around you is good for you. Eat lots of local and seasonal produce instead of packed food. Local and seasonal produce is less likely to be picked off the tree unripe. It is full of nutrients you need based on the climate and geography.

Hack 81: Swap Refined Carbs for Legumes and Whole Grains:

Instead of pasta, eat dhal. Serve your fish or meat with a side of beans. The market is full of healthy and ancient grains from all over the world, like quinoa, millet, barley, bulgur, buckwheat, and amaranth. Some are actually superfoods. Have fun exploring new flavors and recipes.

Hack 82: Fast:

Practice some form of fasting regularly, time-restricted eating (or intermittent fasting).

Hack 83: Signs of an Unhealthy Gut:

Many symptoms, seemingly unrelated to the gut, may indicate an imbalance. These are common ways that an unhealthy gut manifests:

- Digestive issues, food intolerances: A healthy gut has less difficulty processing food and eliminating waste. Upset, stomach, gas, bloating, constipation, diarrhea, heartburn, and nausea can be signs of an imbalance. There is also evidence that food allergies may be related to gut health.

- Skin problems: Gut inflammation increases the "leaking" of certain proteins into the body that irritate the skin and cause skin conditions like eczema.
- Sugar cravings: Processed foods and added sugars can decrease good bacteria, increasing sugar cravings that damage the gut further.
- Unexplained weight changes: Gaining or losing weight without modifying diet or exercise habits may indicate that the gut does not absorb nutrients, regulate blood sugar, or store fat properly.
- Sleep disruptions: Gut damage can impair one's ability to sleep well, even increase the risk for fibromyalgia.
- Chronic fatigue: Certain biomarkers in gut bacteria have been linked to Chronic Fatigue Syndrome. They trigger inflammation, affect the central nervous and immune systems, causing tiredness, pain, poor concentration, memory loss, etc.
- Autoimmune conditions: An unhealthy gut increases systemic inflammation and disrupts the immune system, leading to autoimmune disorders, where the body attacks itself rather than harmful invaders.

Hack 84: Restore Gut Flora When Taking Antibiotics:

Restore proper digestion and absorption using probiotics with a high number of colony-forming units (CFUs) and digestive enzymes.

Hack 85: Tips for Gut Health:

Although we have covered these already, the following list can serve as an easy reference:

- Consume a whole-food, plant-based diet rich in fruits, vegetables, fermented foods, and nuts (especially almonds). Sleep, rest, and de-stress. Limit alcohol. Avoid artificial sweeteners, refined sugars, processed foods, farmed fish and meat, and gluten.

Hack 86: Improve Metabolic Flexibility:

To accomplish this, begin with the following:

- Exercise and resistance training. High-intensity workouts and lifting weights will help your body select the right fuel for the job.
- Cut down on carbs. Eliminate refined grains and sugar. Eat high-quality complex carbs. Add more fiber-rich food.

- Consume good fats and proteins.
- Practice regular intermittent fasting. This is discussed in detail in the next chapter.
- Practice fasted activity. This means exercising on an empty stomach.

Hack 87: Ensure You Have a High BMR:

Begin by finding what your BMR is. Use one of the many calculators on the Internet, making sure that they factor in activity level for the most accurate reading. This will provide a baseline if you have specific goals, like weight loss.

- Eat a relatively protein-rich diet. Proteins are hard for the body to break down; therefore, it burns more calories in the process.
- Eat high-quality carbs.
- Add spice to your food.
- Capsaicin, a compound found in spices like jalapeño and cayenne, stimulate your body to release more adrenaline, speeding up your metabolism.
- Add resistance training to your daily routine.
- Get enough sleep. Drink green tea regularly.
- Drink plenty of water – ½ liter of water can increase your BMR by 15-20% for an hour.

Hack 88: 16:8 Fasting:

This approach extends the feeding window to 8 hours, giving enough time to the body to rest and regenerate during sleep without having to break down food from late-night eating. For example, if you eat dinner at 6 PM, no more food until 10 AM.

Hack 89: Say No to Snacking:

Take your three meals a day but stop munching on snacks in-between.

Hack 90: Combine Keto and Intermittent Fasting:

Again, consult with your doctor before trying this hack, but you may be able to jumpstart weight loss by combining a Keto diet with comfortable intermittent fasting like 12:12. Essentially, this means that you limit eating to a specific window and eat a Ketogenic or Paleo diet within that timeframe.

Hack 91: Calculate and Drink Your Optimum Amount Daily:

You know you are drinking enough water if you rarely feel thirsty and your urine is pale yellow, clear, or cloudy. Make a habit of drinking a glass of water with each meal and between meals.
Drink lots before and after exercise. And, of course, whenever you're thirsty. Doctors advise that women drink at least 11 cups per day and men a minimum of 16. Keep in mind that in high temperatures and with physical activity, you should increase your intake. This simple formula will help you find a baseline for your body: Water (in liters) to drink a day = Your Weight (in Kg) multiplied by 0.033.

Hack 92: Don't Wait Until You Feel Thirsty:

Feeling thirsty is your body's signal that you are already dehydrated. Having a personal water bottle, which you take everywhere, will help you stay hydrated and keep track of your intake. Put your bottle on your nightstand to conveniently sip on, should you wake up at night.

Hack 93: Use an App:

If you are busy and tend to forget, install an app to remind you to drink water throughout the day. Set the goal, and the app will help you achieve it.

Hack 94: Make Better Hydration Choices:

If you love sipping on something throughout the day, replace coffee and sugary drinks with unsweetened coconut water, herb-infused water, or functional teas that have so many other health benefits, in addition to hydration.

Hack 95: Consult Your Doctor and Find A Coach:

If you have medical conditions, speak to your doctor before you start a new regimen. Exercise, especially when vigorous, can strain the heart, lungs, and joints. Make sure that you do not exacerbate any pre-existing conditions or put yourself at risk. After consulting your doctor, it would be advisable to have a qualified fitness coach design the appropriate routine for your physical condition.

Hack 96: Home Workouts:

If you are unable to go outside or do not want to, you can do these exercises indoors:
- Stretching improves flexibility and range of motion. It also improves blood circulation.
- Walk or jog around your garden or terrace.
- Jumping rope is of the best exercises you can do at home.
- Squats and lunges keep you fit and tone your muscles.
- When you first start, ask someone to monitor you; you need to do them correctly to get maximum benefits.
- Jumping jacks are easy to do even in small spaces.

Start any new routine slowly and increase the duration gradually. It may be more effective to break it down into shorter intervals. The Harvard School of Public Health indicates that three 10-minute sessions were as good as one longer session. Remember always to warm up to avoid injury.

Hack 97: Tips to Stay Active:

If you despise working out, and nothing can convince you to hit the gym, these suggestions will help you remain active:
- Walk everywhere: If your destination is very far away, take public transport part of the way or park at a distance. Listening to music while walking improves mood. Impact forces on the feet can total several hundred tons, so invest in quality footwear. If you can't wear sneakers all day, bring a change of shoes with you.
- Take the stairs: Stair climbing is considered the ultimate calorie burner. It's also great cardio.
- Cook and clean: Sweeping and mopping are great workouts. A 150-pound person can burn between 85-102 calories per half-hour by cleaning. They can burn up to 78 calories in 30 minutes of cooking! As a bonus, home-cooked food is always healthier because you control the ingredients.
- Dance: Dancing burns around 200 calories every half-hour.
- Mind and body: If you prefer or require low-impact exercise, consider Yoga, Pilates, and Tai Chi. You will move your body and practice mindfulness at the same time.

Hack 98: Use Apps:

Use a fitness app or wearable to track how many steps you have taken each day to reach your goals. Set reminders so you can get up from your desk and move around at regular intervals. Studies show that moving every 30 minutes can minimize the negative effects of a sedentary lifestyle.

Hack 99: Tips for a Good Night's Sleep:

Simple, easy, everyday suggestions to maximize the quality of your sleep:

Avoid eating 2–3 hours before bedtime. Avoid caffeine and alcohol, especially close to bedtime. Sleep in a dark, quiet, and cool room. Invest in a quality mattress and pillows. Remove all electronic devices from the bedroom. A shower or bath before bed relaxes your body and makes you feel like you have washed the day away. Get regular exercise during the day. Avoid tobacco. If your partner's snoring prevents you from sleeping, address their problem as well. If your mind is racing about the things you have to do the next day, making a schedule might put your mind at ease.

Hack 100: Dealing with Insomnia:

If you have chronic insomnia, seek professional advice. If it's an occasional problem, in addition to the above tips, the following may help:

- After trying to fall asleep for 20 minutes, get up and read, then try again later. There are many prescription and over-the-counter sleep aids, but first, try a functional tea like chamomile or lavender to help you unwind. If you need something to put you to sleep, try a valerian root tea.
- Switch to a whole-food, plant-based diet rich in fruit, vegetables, legumes, nuts, and whole grains.
- Try sleep restriction therapy, which reduces the time spent in bed to match your sleep hours closely. It is often used with stimulus control therapy, which strengthens the association between bed and sleep by using the bed only for sleep and sex.
- Breathing and muscle relaxation techniques can improve sleep quality. Create a bedtime ritual – this may involve showering, drinking a functional tea, preparing your space for sleep, meditating, etc.

Hack 101: Problems and Solutions:

There are many reasons why meditation does not come easily to everyone. Here, we address the most common obstacles.

- "I can't clear my mind." If you have a "monkey mind," try mindfulness meditation, which makes you fully aware of your thoughts in the present moment.
- "I get restless." If you find it impossible to sit still, try a moving meditation.
- "I can't do the lotus posture." Then don't! Sit on a chair or lie down. What's important is that you are comfortable enough to unwind.
- "I don't have enough time." If you cannot spare time during the day, then do it before you fall asleep or as soon as you wake up in the morning.
- "I fall asleep." Stretch beforehand and meditate sitting up. Do it during a time of day when you are most alert.
- "I can't stick with it." Yes, but you can start again today. Don't just quit; keep trying.
- "I won't be good at it." Many people doubt themselves and give up. Practice makes perfect.

Hack 102: Find the Best Practice for You:

Start by identifying your goals. Are you looking for spiritual growth, improved concentration, or relaxation? Keep in mind that you can practice several forms for different reasons.

Hack 103: Create a Sanctuary:

If you design a beautiful, quiet, private, and comfortable space, not only will you be eager to retreat there but also get into the mood more quickly. A comfortable chair or daybed, plush pillows, incense, crystals, music, art, even your personal altar will help.

Hack 104: Apps, Guided Meditations, Binaural Beats:

These work well for beginners, especially if you have difficulty relaxing or clearing your mind.

Hack 105: Simple Breathing Techniques:

Lengthen your exhale for stress release. When you feel agitated, stop what you are doing, and take a deep breath. However, taking too many deep breaths too quickly can cause you to hyperventilate. Before you take a deep breath, push all the air out of your lungs, and then let them do their work. To center yourself, simply observe your breath without trying to control it. Focus your attention on the air passing to your lungs, feeling the expansion in your chest and belly. Diaphragmatic breathing reduces the work your body needs to do and maximizes oxygenation.

Hack 106: Mind-Body Synergy

The following suggestions summarize what we have discussed in this section while adding a few elements.

- **Fundamentals:** These are diet and gut health, hydration, sleep, and active lifestyle.
- **Fasting:** Research shows that a 12% caloric restriction decreased the risk of many fatal diseases. Intermittent fasting has also proven to be very helpful.
- **Organics and supplements:** Even if you avoid processed foods, industrialized food is nutritionally depleted and contains harmful chemicals like pesticides. Eat organic as often as possible, especially when it comes to functional herbs and supplements because their therapeutic benefits will be potent and complete. Take supplements as needed, like Vitamin D in winter if you live in a cold climate where sunlight is unavailable daily.
- **Oxygenation:** Tel Aviv University and Shamir Medical Centre found that Hyperbaric Oxygen Therapy reversed critical indicators of aging. You may not have access to an oxygen chamber like Michael Jackson but can maximize oxygenation with breathwork. Clean air will do wonders for your mind and body – get as much as you can.
- **Mind over matter:** Your body is always listening to your words and thoughts. If you believe that you will deteriorate with age, it will create that reality. Using visualizations, guided meditations, and affirmations, you can communicate anti-aging instructions to your body.

Hack 107: Safe Biohacking:

Although some forms of biohacking are extreme and risky, the term simply means making changes to optimize the way the body functions. There are two ways to try it safely and effectively:

- For specific health concerns, biohacking can mean treating the problem, not only the symptoms. Instead of relying only on allopathic medicine to manage the issue, explore alternative healing modalities. If you are healthy, you can test your body's responses to specific changes, thereby finding natural ways to improve the way you feel. Biohacks include strategies like trying an elimination or raw food diet.

Hack 108: Stay in The Moment:

Most of us tend to live in our past or future, defining ourselves by our memories or expectations. We hold on to past hurts and fear future loss, but the past is gone and the future unknown. Learning to live in the present is the only way to stop being haunted by things you have no control over; focus on the 'now moment'. It's the only thing that is real.

Hack 109: Create a Gratitude Journal:

Research shows that developing an attitude of gratefulness transforms individuals and societies for the better. Create a gratitude journal and write in it before going to bed. Make a habit of appreciating at least one small thing every day. Training your mind to observe and value something as simple as a stranger's smile or a glorious sunset will make you a better and happier person.

Hack 110: Forgive, Let Go, and Move On:

Let go of grudges because the only person you are hurting is yourself. The other people are not suffering from the toxic feelings that are within you.

Forgiving does not mean that you are saying that what they did was okay. You do it because you need to feel lighter and focus on things that matter. Also, you can only give to others what you have – if you are filled with anger and resentment, that's what you will project to the world. Make sure you have forgiveness and kindness to share.

Hack 111: Be Brave:

If you are stuck in a relationship, job, or situation that is making you miserable – even if it's just "a thorn in your side" – this prevents you from growing. Be brave enough to go out into the world and seek your happiness.

Hack 112: Do a SWOT Analysis on Yourself:

A term used in business, SWOT is the acronym for strengths, weaknesses, opportunities, and threats. Knowing yourself will make you confident – you will realize you have overcome plenty of obstacles in the past and will continue to do so in the future.

You will identify the areas you need to work on, face the challenges and get out of your comfort zone. It will build a growth mindset that is conducive to happiness.

Hack 113: Shift From "What if?" to "How can I?"

Do you tend to assume that something will go wrong, always asking, "What if...?" If yes, you should realize that most scenarios you create in your head are unlikely to happen. In an article for Psychology Today, Professor Graham C.L. Davey tackles "what-if-worrying" and points out that one must not waste time picturing the worst scenario; instead, one should focus on how the situation can be managed.

The next time you think that something may go wrong, stop yourself and reimagine it going well. You can also weigh a negative outcome in terms of importance. Ask yourself, "Will it matter in five years?" If not, then don't spend more than five minutes on it.

Hack 114: The "I-can-handle-it" Mindset:

Another trick that comes in handy is telling yourself that you'll handle whatever comes your way. This not only gives you a confident disposition but also soothes your mind. Coupled with the "How can I?" hack, this approach will help reduce your stress and become proactive. It's a win-win proposition.

Hack 115: Keep a Worry Diary:

As counter-intuitive as this sounds, it's an excellent approach to sorting out your concerns before they become a tangled mess in your mind. Keeping a worry diary forces you to become conscious of your worries. Note down your thoughts for a week, then separate them into two categories.

Hack 116: Schedule "Worry Time."

As we have seen, constructive concerns can give you ideas and help you prepare. Since humans are hardwired to worry because it ensures their survival, schedule some "worry time." Allot 30 minutes. Don't exceed the limit, and every time you catch yourself worrying other than during the designated period, work on something else. Treat this time as self-care and address your concerns.

Hack 117: Talk It Through:

Worrying can have you going around in a mental loop, especially if you are alone. In such moments, it helps to reach out to a friend – a fresh pair of ears and another mind. Sometimes, all you need is to let it out because that makes acceptance easier.

Empathy and love lead to better mental health and problem-solving. Talking to a compassionate friend will help you sort out your issues effectively. In the case of excessive worrying, you can seek a therapist who can help you manage your stress.

Hack 118: Avoid Suppressing Worries:

The most common advice one receives is, "Don't worry." Sometimes, people think that burying negative thoughts will make them go away. Wishing worries away makes them return with vigor. It is crucial to acknowledge them and move on, as opposed to denying and letting them fester.

Research shows that individuals who are more accepting of intrusive thoughts exhibit lower levels of depression and anxiety. Therefore, acknowledge intrusive thoughts and let go.

Hack 119: Uncertainty Is the Only Certainty:

It is crucial to make peace with change because we know little to nothing about what the future holds. Accepting that nothing is permanent will help reduce anxiety. Prepare for different possibilities by making plans and being confident about your coping mechanisms instead of having expectations.

Hack 120: Be Mindful, and Here's How:

Mindfulness means being aware of yourself and your surroundings. Mindfulness meditation is used to alleviate stress and anxiety by directing your attention elsewhere when you're plagued with negative thoughts.

To put it into practice, follow these steps:

Practice paying attention to your body and its sensations, for instance, the flavor of your toothpaste while brushing your teeth. Try to live in the moment and experience life's simple pleasures. Accept yourself wholeheartedly, warts and all. Believe that you are unique and valuable. Focus on your breathing for at least two minutes every day. After you have practiced the above, regularly perform a body scan, along with sitting or walking meditations to lighten your mind and body. Sitting meditation is essentially lying on your back with extended limbs and palms facing up. Or, sit comfortably on the floor with folded legs and breathing in and out. Focus on each part of the body and feel the sensations. Similarly, choose a quiet spot of about 20 feet for a walking meditation and walk across it while intensely focusing on the sensations.

Hack 121: Say Yes, More Often:

Say yes to things that interest you. For example, attend a seminar outside the scope of your work. You might learn something that opens you to new ideas. Say yes to things that bring you joy, like calling an old friend. Bond over a coffee, vent, or relive memories you shared. A conversation will surely make you feel good.

Hack 122: Resist the Mundane:

Slowly drop humdrum activities from your day, like TV and doom scrolling. Instead, join a book club even if you're not a voracious reader. Spontaneity is about breaking routines.

Hack 123: Just Do It:

Stop daydreaming about this or that exciting thing. Act spontaneously at least once a week. It could be as simple as a walk in the park or as adventurous as a trip to Goa.

Hack 124: Take Calculated Risks:

Foster growth by getting out of your comfort zone and challenging yourself. Take at least one risk a month, like investing a small sum in a new stock.

Hack 125: Break Rules:

Break the rules without infringing on someone else's rights. If there's a chance that you can experience something new, then do so.

Hack 126: Increase Stillness and Reduce Distractions:

Begin by scheduling stillness time, a few minutes first thing in the morning before your prayers, exercise, or breakfast. Also, gradually reduce the time you spend around external stimuli, like screens for entertainment purposes.

Hack 127: Speak Less:

Avoid speaking unless necessary, especially about insignificant things.

Consciously practice being quiet for at least 20 minutes a day. Before bed, spend at least 15 minutes quietly doing and thinking nothing. This helps reduce the chatter in your mind and ensures you fall asleep quickly.

Hack 128: Take Up a Regular Meditative Practice:

Whether that means meditation, Yoga, Tai Chi, or going for a hike, set aside a time when you can go inward. This will help you de-stress, giving you plenty of time to introspect.

Hack 129: Breathe:

A critical component in calming the body and mind is breathing, especially during stressful moments. Take slow, deep breaths to slow your heart rate – this works well if you experience anxiety.

Hack 130: Mind Your Manners:

A nice word or gesture can make someone's day because they feel acknowledged. Whether you smile at a cashier or give your seat to someone on the bus, you uplift and assist in the simplest of ways.

Hack 131: Donate and Share:

In addition to money, you can donate clothing, food, time, skills, books, and so on. The idea is to give or share something useful. *"Thousands of candles can be lit from a single candle, and the life of the candle will not be shortened,"* said the Buddha.

Hack 132: Serve and Show Love:

"If you can't feed a hundred people, then feed one," urged Mother Teresa. You can assist a sick neighbor or visit shelters and orphanages – play games with the kids, read to the elders, and serve food to the homeless. Remember, most of them are either abandoned or have no family. Assure them that they are not alone and that they can reach out to you. However, always make sure to step up when they need you. Fake promises might worsen the emotional trauma.

Hack 133: Focus on the Good; Do Not Judge:

As previously indicated, a contribution is most impactful when it comes from the heart, both for the one who gives and for the one who receives. Look for the good in others, even if you don't see it clearly at first. Always put yourself in the other person's shoes before judging them. Although the world is filled with negativity, stay positive – this way, you are doubling your gift by giving both material things and hope.

Hack 134: Aim for Long-Term Impact:

I cannot stress the importance of this Chinese proverb enough, *"Give a man a fish; you feed him to fish for a day. Teach him how to fish. You feed him for a lifetime."* When giving, look for projects with lasting benefits. Yes, it's imperative to send people food and medicine in an emergency.

However, your money would transform lives if you bought a goat for a family or helped build a well for clean water in a developing country.

Hack 135: Speak Up:

Change can only take place if enough people raise their voices. If Greta Thunberg had stayed silent, we would not have had the greatest climate strike in history. Other young girls, inspired by Greta, have started measures in their own countries. The point is, one person can make a difference, but a group can bring about a change.

Of course, the goal does not have to be that grand. If a person is being bullied at work, speak up in their defense. You don't have to be confrontational; subtly point out to the bully that their behavior is inappropriate. For example, you can say, "Hey, I felt uncomfortable about how you spoke to that person."

Hack 136: One Small Act of Kindness A Day:

"Three things in human life are important. The first is to be kind. The second is to be kind. And the third is to be kind," Henry James sums up so perfectly. Here are a few things you can practice to make compassion your default setting:

- Do your best not to get angry with people. Never insult them; if you must give critical feedback, make sure it's constructive and expressed with respect. Everybody makes mistakes, even you! If someone asks for help, give them a hand. Build up your good karma credits.
- If you hold a high position in society, stay humble. Talk to people; let them know they can reach out to you in times of need. Be sociable and approachable; this is an ecosystem. *"You can be, should be, and need to be involved in the world. It truly needs you,"* writes Elaine N. Aron. Being involved does not mean interfering in other people's lives. It means making yourself available, open, and receptive. If they need your opinion, a shoulder to cry on, or an ear to listen, they can reach out to you.

- Strive to be a role model, especially for youth. Teach by example and practice what you preach. Start changing yourself to see the ripple effect around you.

REFERENCES

FINDING YOUR LIFE PURPOSE

1. https://www.jackcanfield.com/store/the-success-principles-10th-anniversary-edition/
2. https://marianne.com/a-return-to-lo

SETTING A GRAND VISION FOR YOUR LIFE

1. https://en.wikipedia.org/wiki/Predictions_made_by_Ray_Kurzwe
2. https://www.rethinkx.com/transportation

GETTING IN THE FLOW

1. https://www.headspace.com/articles/flow-state
2. https://www.verywellmind.com/what-is-flow-2794768
3. https://www.youtube.com/watch?v=WqAtG77JjdM&ab_channel=TEDxTalks

CULTIVATING THE ABUNDANCE MINDSET

1. https://futuristspeaker.com/business-trends/33-dramatic-predictions-for-2030/

BEING AN IDEA MACHINE

1. https://jamesaltucher.com/blog/the-ultimate-guide-for-becoming-an-idea-machine/
2. https://www.chriswinfield.com/ideas/
3. https://medium.com/@rgeddes/are-you-an-idea-guy-907cd10bb253
4. https://prowritingaid.com/art/26/10-Free-Writing-Apps-and-Tools.aspx

BEING PRODUCTIVE

1. https://www.investopedia.com/terms/p/productivity.asp
2. https://www.robinsharma.com/article/the-sword-crafter-s-parable-a-quick-story-about-productivity
3. https://www.nytimes.com/guides/business/how-to-improve-your-productivity-at-work
4. https://www.forbes.com/sites/nomanazish/2018/06/18/10-incredibly-easy-ways-to-improve-your-productivity/#440c0058365b

INTEGRITY IS THE WAY OF LIFE

1. https://www.entrepreneur.com/article/235267
2. https://www.success.com/9-tips-to-help-you-strengthen-your-integr

MASTERING YOUR HABITS

1. https://www.merriam-webster.com/dictionary/habit
2. https://www.inverse.com/mind-body/the-truth-about-making-breaking-habits/amp
3. https://www.nytimes.com/2019/03/25/smarter-living/why-you-procrastinate-it-has-nothing-to-do-with-self-control.html
4. https://ideas.ted.com/what-old-story-about-yourself-are-you-still-believing-heres-how-to-find-it-and-change-it/
5. https://www.inverse.com/mind-body/the-character-edge-why-competence-isnt-enough-for-great-leadership/amp
6. https://blog.cheapism.com/unhealthy-habits/amp/
7. https://www.researchgate.net/publication/228071867
8. https://journals.sagepub.com/doi/abs/10.1177/0146167207311201
9. https://jamesclear.com/new-habit
10. https://jamesclear.com/habits.

MINDING YOUR WORDS

1. https://www.youtube.com/watch?v=c-uSqm05RrM&feature=youtu.be
2. https://www.psychologytoday.com/us/blog/inviting-monkey-tea/201809/mindful-speech-using-your-words-help-not-harm
3. https://www.yogitimes.com/article/austerity-of-speech-bhagavad-gita-spirituality
4. https://www.yogajournal.com/philosophy/talk-pretty/
5. https://www.youtube.com/watch?v=03FsTbkcxuI&feature=youtu.be
6. https://www.youtube.com/watch?v=MlDnhQl1VEQ&feature=youtu.be

BEING ATTRACTIVE

1. https://theartofsimple.net/10-ways-to-instantly-become-more-attractive/
2. https://www.scienceofpeople.com/attraction/

MONEY FUNDAMENTALS

1. https://www.tonyrobbins.com/business/money-management/
2. https://www.get-rich-and-retire-early.com/thinking-like-rich/
3. https://www.etmoney.com/blog/what-is-financial-freedom-and-ways-to-achieve-it/
4. https://www.jimrohn.com/3-money-habits-separate-rich-poor/
5. https://www.chime.com/blog/4-inspiring-stories-to-motivate-you-to-become-more-financially-literate/

SPEND vs. SAVE vs. INTEREST

1. https://www.businessinsider.com/personal-finance/when-to-save-money-vs-spend-money-improve-life
2. https://www.discover.com/credit-cards/resources/spending-vs-saving/
3. https://www.investopedia.com/stocks-4427785
4. https://www.nerdwallet.com/blog/investing/invest-stocks-etfs-mutual-funds/

BEING ASSET-LIGHT

1. https://www.business-standard.com/article/news-ani/companies-that-run-successful-on-asset-light-model-118072800246_
2. https://agileleanlife.com/asset-light-living/
3. https://www.youtube.com/watch?v=D-qgMb15M1w&ab_channel=SuccessResources
4. https://www.thebalancesmb.com/the-sharing-economy-
5. https://www.diamandis.com/blog/predicting-the-next-10-years

INCREASING YOUR EARNING POTENTIAL

1. http://press.careerbuilder.com/2017-08-24-Living-Paycheck-to-Paycheck-is-a-Way-of-Life-for-Majority-of-U-S-Workers-According-to-New-CareerBuilder-Survey
2. https://investinganswers.com/articles/how-become-financially-independent-5-years-or-less
3. https://www.mrmoneymustache.com/2012/01/13/the-shockingly-simple-math-behind-early-retirement/
4. https://thecollegeinvestor.com/16399/20-passive-income-ideas/
5. https://twocents.lifehacker.com/the-basics-of-fire-financial-independence-and-early-re-1820129768

BEING VALUABLE

1. https://www.entrepreneur.com/article/236807
2. https://www.inc.com/peter-economy/9-questions-to-rate-your-value-to-the-organization.html

3. https://www.thebalancecareers.com/how-to-make-yourself-more-valuable-to-your-boss-4027557
4. https://www.amanet.org/articles/fifteen-ways-to-show-your-value-at-work/
5. https://www.inc.com/kevin-daum/35-habits-that-make-employees-extremely-valuable.html

BEING SERVICE MINDED

1. https://yourbusiness.azcentral.com/strategies-tactics-exemplary-customer-service-14734.html
2. https://cloudcherry.com/blog/4e-cultivating-service-mindset/
3. https://www.success.com/serve-others-to-get-all-you-want/
4. https://digitalcommons.unomaha.edu/cgi/viewcontent
5. https://www.briantracy.com/blog/sales-success/using-the-law-of-reciprocity-and-other-persuasion-techniques-correctly/
6. http://www.businessfranchiseaustralia.com.au/expert-advice/6-service-mindsets-achieve-positive-service-culture

BEING A CONSUMMATE PROFESSIONAL

1. https://careertrend.com/displaying-professional-attitude-8820.html
2. https://www.entrepreneur.com/article/253095
3. https://smallbusiness.chron.com/five-attitudes-important-workplaces-19114.html
4. https://www.dailyleader.com/2017/08/18/attitude-more-important-than-skills/

BEING VISIBLE

1. https://www.mindtools.com/pages/article/increasing-visibility.htm
2. https://www.forbes.com/sites/elenabajic/2015/07/28/7-ways-to-raise-your-visibility-and-advance-your-career/?sh=45a665d14ff1
3. https://www.themuse.com/advice/5-5minute-ways-to-get-noticed-at-work-by-the-people-who-matter
4. https://eatyourcareer.com/2018/06/raise-visibility-work/
5. https://www.thebalancecareers.com/how-to-raise-your-visibility-at-work-1919217

DEVELOPING AN ENTREPRENEURIAL MINDSET

1. https://www.lifehack.org/535083/how-does-entrepreneurial-mindset-help-you-life
2. https://www.fastcompany.com/3030817/how-to-think-like-an-entrepreneur-even-when-youre-not-one
3. https://www.gmac.com/why-gmac/gmac-news/gmnews/2017/february-2017/think-like-an-entrepreneur

4. https://www.entrepreneur.com/article/250480

FUTURE-PROOFING YOURSELF

1. https://su.org/blog/exponential-technology-trends-defined-2019/
2. https://hbrascend.org/topics/the-4-essential-skills-to-future-proof-your-career/
3. https://www.roberthalf.com/blog/the-future-of-work/strategies-to-future-proof-your-career
4. https://www.fastcompany.com/90445947/how-to-future-proof-your-career-path-in-2020-and-beyond
5. https://www.mindtools.com/pages/article/newCDV_81.htm

ENVIRONMENTAL POLLUTION AND TOXICITY

1. https://daveasprey.com/my-flood-story-and-what-to-do-about-mold/

DIET

1. https://www.who.int/news-room/fact-sheets/detail/healthy-diet
2. https://www.medicalnewstoday.com/articles/5847#1-atkins-diet

GUT HEALTH

1. https://www.eatthe80.com/love-your-gut-why-a-healthy-gut-is-so-important/
2. https://neurosciencenews.com/depression-microbiome-brain-function-17414/

FASTING AND AUTOPHAGY

1. https://www.healthline.com/health/autophagy#bottom-line
2. https://naomiw.com/blogs/nutrition/the-12-important-benefits-of-autophagy
3. https://naomiw.com/blogs/nutrition/autophagy-your-most-pressing-questions-answered
4. https://drmindypelz.com/top-5-foods-that-stimulate-autophagy/

HYDRATION

1. https://www.hsph.harvard.edu/news/hsph-in-the-news/the-importance-of-hydration/
2. https://rhitrition.com/how-much-water-should-drink-every-day/

ACTIVE LIFESTYLE

1. http://themocracy.com/the-importance-of-living-an-active-lifestyle/
2. https://www.downtoearth.org.in/news/health/india-has-the-second-higest-number-of-obese-children-in-the-world-58115
3. Luhar S, Timæus IM, Jones R, et al. Forecasting the prevalence of overweight and obesity in India to 2040. PLoS One. 2020;15(2):e0229438. Published 2020 Feb 24. doi:10.1371/journal.pone.0229438
4. https://www.everydayhealth.com/fitness-pictures/ways-to-stay-active-all-day.aspx
5. https://www.healthline.com/health/womens-health-active-lifestyle

MEDITATION

1. https://www.dhamma.org/en/about/vipassana
2. https://www.indiatoday.in/lifestyle/health/story/what-exactly-is-vipassana-the-meditation-technique-president-kovind-swears-by-1145720-2018-01-15
3. https://en.wikipedia.org/wiki/Silva_Method

BREATHWORK

1. https://lonerwolf.com/mindfulness-practices/

LONGEVITY AND AGING BACKWARDS

1. https://www.independent.co.uk/life-style/gadgets-and-tech/anti-ageing-reverse-treatment-telomeres-b1748067.html
2. https://www.successpodcast.com/show-notes/2020/7/30/how-to-stop-amp-reverse-aging-with-dr-david-sinclair
3. Image: Kennedy BK, Berger SL, Brunet A, Campisi J, Cuervo AM, Epel ES, Franceschi C, Lithgow GJ, Morimoto RI, Pessin JE, Rando TA, Richardson A, Schadt EE, Wyss-Coray T, Sierra F. Geroscience: linking aging to chronic disease. Cell. 2014 Nov 6;159(4):709-13. doi: 10.1016/j.cell.2014.10.039. PMID: 25417146; PMCID: PMC4852871.
4. https://mariashriver.com/bulletproof-founder-dave-asprey-on-biohacking-and-why-well-all-live-past-100/

HAPPINESS AND FULFILLMENT

1. https://dictionary.apa.org/happiness
2. Bono, Giacomo & Emmons, Robert & Mccullough, Michael. (2012). Gratitude in Practice and the Practice of Gratitude. 10.1002/9780470939338.ch23.
3. https://greatergood.berkeley.edu/topic/happiness/definition#how-cultivate-happiness
4. Dunn, Elizabeth & Aknin, Lara & Norton, Michael. (2008). Spending

Money on Others Promotes Happiness. Science (New York, N.Y.). 319. 1687-8. 10.1126/science.1150952

PRACTICING BENEFICIAL WORRYING

1. https://www.tuw.edu/health/how-stress-affects-the-brain/
2. https://www.psychologytoday.com/us/blog/why-we-worry/201206/10-tips-manage-your-worrying
3. https://www.huffingtonpost.in/entry/stop-worrying-anxiety-cycle_n_4002914?ri18n=true
4. https://tinybuddha.com/blog/7-ways-to-deal-with-uncertainty/

BEING SPONTANEOUS

1. https://www.calmmoment.com/well-being/why-being-spontaneous-can-make-us-happier/
2. https://www.kindspring.org/story/view.php?sid=31763
3. https://www.scotthyoung.com/blog/2008/02/21/7-tips-to-live-a-more-spontaneous-life/

BEING STILL

1. https://michaelhyatt.com/the-practice-of-stillness/
2. https://alltimeshortstories.com/inspirational-story-the-power-of-silence/
3. https://psychcentral.com/blog/the-power-in-being-still-how-to-practice-stillness/

MAKING A DIFFERENCE

1. https://www.forbes.com/sites/margiewarrell/2018/12/08/why-doing-good-is-ultimate-success-strategy/#679a89bb6478
2. https://lifebeyondnumber

AFTERWORD

I believe that discontentment is not our lot as human beings; we have been programmed to accept this distorted worldview because it serves those who instilled it. At this time in history, we have ideas and technologies that can birth a brighter tomorrow. I believe that, now, the "I can't" mindset can be overwritten by "I can" more easily. Yes, we have weaknesses but also the strength to overcome them. I believe that we have within ourselves everything we need to embody our highest purpose. And that doing so is our God-given birthright.

If I did not believe these things, I would not have drafted this roadmap to thriving. It is neither conclusive nor complete, and it can never be because each person must walk their unique path.

Still, I hope that my efforts will help you live your life to the fullest, whether you are twenty, forty, or eighty. Carpe diem. It's never too late to be happy and fulfilled...

– Ravikummar

ABOUT THE AUTHOR

Ravikummar M currently serves as the Senior Vice President at NTT Data, a multinational IT Services, and Consulting company headquartered in Tokyo, Japan. In his current capacity, Ravikummar has the privilege of leading over 10,000 young and enthusiastic professionals. He started as a Software Programmer and gradually climbed up the ladder to create a niche for himself.

His outstanding efforts and path-breaking initiatives contributed to shaping the India delivery centers, which are a significant component of NTT DATA's success. Under his leadership, successful growth and transformation emerged through strategic and creative insights for developing delivery infrastructure, to mentoring and nurturing blossoming talents, and ultimately contributing towards building innovation and competency centers. With creativity and efficiency, Mr. Kumar continues to leave an indelible mark with each contribution to the continued growth and success of the company and industry.

Ravikummar believes in living life deliberately, on purpose, being a student of life, and helping people maximize their potential. He is a prolific speaker and has spoken to thousands of audiences across different parts of the world. This book is the result of his lifelong learning from his mentors and his experience of working with people from all walks of life. Ravikummar completed his Bachelor's in Mechanical Engineering from UBDT College of Engineering, Karnataka, India. He also holds a Masters in Technology from the National Institute of Karnataka, India.

- Check out www.thrivinghacks.com, www.living-on-purpose.net,
- Follow @ThrivingHacks on Facebook, @ThrivingHacks on Twitter, and @ThrivingHacks on Instagram.